Dedicated to two extraordinary men:
my father, Roger Chapin, and
my father-in-law, Dominic Skaperdas.

Contents

Nature Spirits

Life After Life

Tears are words that need to be written.

—Paulo Coelho

Foreword

As a psychologist in the field of grief, loss, and trauma for over four decades, I have investigated ancient wisdom, somatic practices, and emerging developmental neuroscience for therapeutic practices for people suffering severe losses. On reading this book, my respect for the therapeutic practice of reflective writing has deepened. Reflective writing arises directly from the inner world and bypasses analytical problem solving to resolve interrupted emotional processing. Many of the writers in the book describe how their experience began in hurt, chaos, and confusion and was gradually transformed into new meaning for their lives.

Grief is a complex process that involves radical changes in our inner world and in the ordinary interactions we share with others. When grief is denied, thwarted, or interrupted, the intense emotions needed to redirect our life are negated. When unprocessed, these powerful feelings accumulate in the body and become trauma, a state of emotional and physical illness. Without time, support, and an intimate knowledge of our own grief, our bodies develop "survival reactions" that are triggered by associations or reminders of the loss. Survival reactions are rooted in a chronic disruption of the nervous system, which can lead to physical and emotional illnesses such as immune, digestive, respiratory, and circulatory disorders. Emotional disorders from survival reactions impede intimacy; foster a sense of disconnection and depression; and fuel fatigue, stress, chronic anger, and anxiety issues.

My own experiences of loss, grief, trauma, and death have convinced me of the importance of paying attention to physical feelings, emotions, and visuals in order for the transformation to occur. The writers in this book recognize that they know instinctively what they need to do to heal as well as the relational support they need from others.

Healing occurs with the compassionate empathy between a griever and a listener. When a writer explores their own lived experience, they take on a dual perspective, the observing witness as well as the person experiencing suffering. As the writers probe and become more aware of the hidden elements of their lived experience, they are able to observe their own lives with empathy and compassion.

In *The Secret Life of Objects*, Toti O'Brien recalls how her mother replaced direct emotional nurturing with jewelry. For Toti, the gifts of jewelry from her mother were meaningless objects. Throughout her life, Toti struggled to connect through objects rather than the gaze, voice, and touch that are essential for emotional relationships. When Toti lost and then found a gift of jewelry from her mother, she reflected on how things can be simply hidden and then found. With this awareness, Toti recognized the connection with her mother that had been hidden by the objects. She realized that her mother did love her but did not have the skills to communicate this directly. So many of us struggle with the inability to let the cherished people in our lives know how much we love them and to recognize that we may not know how much others love us. Grief feels like disconnection and, as Toti discovered, the connection was simply hidden from view.

Healthy grieving ultimately requires a release of conscious control and a surrender into the reality of the present moment. In order to surrender to reality, we need emotional awareness and connection. In a number of the stories, the writers describe a meaningful resolution when they bring compassion to their own authentic suffering.

In *Wake-up Call*, Aubrey Montoya grieves the loss of adequate nurturing by her mother when Aubrey is a young child. Early losses of nurturing from caregivers predict survival reactions. Aubrey's survival reactions include a pregnancy at fifteen, suicide ideation, and anger at her mother's broken promises. As a writer, Aubrey brings painful memories into full awareness. When she is able to feel her pain and acknowledge her suffering, her undifferentiated grief begins to open, and new emotional connections are forged. Aubrey's reflections on her awareness lead her to a deep sense of purpose in parenting her son. Aubrey's recollections begin with an awareness of her inner world, despite pain, anguish, and loneliness. This kind of awareness requires courage, persistence, and a profound hope in healing. Awareness of the inner world includes the perceptions, bodily based sensations, emotions, and images that constitute memories. An inquiry into these memories is different than assessing facts; for Aubrey it was a fearless exploration of the body, mind, and heart. Her relationships with grief empowered her to explore memories with compassion and inner wisdom as she discovered who she was and the possible purpose in her life despite significant loss. As human beings we have two distinct memory systems, implicit and explicit. Implicit memories appear in the form of sensory fragments, such as a general feeling in our body or barely perceptible images. Explicit memories have more structure, sequence, and clarity. The reconnection of implicit, bodily based memories and explicit, autobiographical memories is necessary to heal unresolved trauma. The more we can feel our memories and recall the details, the more fluidly we move through the grieving process. Both the implicit and explicit memories tell the story of our lives; they record the small interactions that create and nourish relationships or reveal the absence of caring and connection.

These two memory systems are integrated in Wendy Staley Colbert's *Splitsville or Bust*. Following a diagnosis of breast cancer, Wendy's husband, Mark, says and does the right things. However, Wendy senses his emotional absence. She recognizes his unspoken preference for a younger woman. In an effort to recapture Mark's affection, Wendy explores the possibility of reconstructive surgery despite higher survival-risk. As she does so she realizes that she has begun to distance herself from her own body. Her surgical choices become clear as she returns to her primary relationship with her own body.

Grief can be felt as a loss of physical presence. In *Paying to Sleep Alone*, Laura Hart describes her professional service of sleeping with lonely people. The need for another body to fill an empty space exposes how vulnerable we all are to loneliness deep within the soul. Laura reveals that her own loneliness has brought her to this work.

Throughout this book, writers demonstrate an integrative processing of grief that moves from chaotic loss to new meaning. Writing is an opportunity to recall, explore, integrate, and reconnect diverse elements that form our memories. Diana Raab describes the shared bond through writing that was forged when she explored her grandmother's journals. In those journals, she discovered horrific childhood trauma at the roots of her grandmother's depression. Research in the field of multi-generational trauma and epigenetics explains how unresolved grief of our ancestors can be retained in our bodies and then passed down to our children. In *The Red Book*, C.G. Jung suggests that the living are called to lament the dead, to resolve that which has been unprocessed by those who came before us. With her exploration of her own life and her grandmother's journals, Diana comes into a deeper understanding and acceptance of her own life.

Stephen Mead likens his process of grieving to the practice of saying the rosary, where the prayer involves pondering images and words that arise in awareness from random memories. After some time, these beads of emotion, words, and thought form into the poetry that expresses his unique perspective.

Memories, both implicit and explicit, recognize the existence of legacy, the tangible and intangible gifts passed on from parent to child and in other significant relationships. Dane Chapin recalls his memories of his "Pop" and his legacy of an "examined life." Loraine Wolff recalls how she was able to provide her spouse with the gift of dying at home. She describes an appreciation of the intimacy and small interactions that can occur between two people. When describing a teacher's legacy, Bret Stephens recalls Mrs. Kass, the teacher who "shaped souls." Respect in a classroom was achieved when the "tone was set by the way we addressed one another." Andrea Adams creates a vivid image of the artful bed-making skills she learned from her grandmother. Her recollections triggered my own memory of my father lovingly placing newspapers between my bedcovers during the freezing nights of my childhood. Blankets were in short supply in our household, but caring and mindfulness was plentiful. Highly valued legacies involve tender awareness of the often hidden yet simple aspects of life.

Each of the stories and poems in this book reveals unique glimpses into the complex kaleidoscope of the human experience of memory, love, loss, grief, and trauma. The contributions of each writer have touched me with the simplicity of what we need for an emotionally healthy and meaningful life. For each of us, it is essential to open our awareness to memories that emerge, whether implicit in the form of vague sensory fragments, moods, or images, or explicit in terms of loss, separation, and disconnection. As you will see in this anthology, when people begin to write about their unprocessed lived experience, something is radically changed. We do not alter the past with our recollections, but we revise our perspective. Reflective writing brings that which is usually invisible to the surface for contemplation. Like Toti, we discover hidden resources within our inner world and in our relationships. These resources transform our relationship with the past, enhance our aliveness in the present, and strengthen our hopes for the future. The human experience of love involves both pain and loss; the exploration of memories, despite the pain and sorrow, challenges us toward growth and meaning in surprising ways.

Sharon Stanley, PhD

Introduction

I am one of those fortunate sons who can say that my father was also my best friend. After he passed away from a difficult and debilitating illness—which I thought for sure he would conquer—I was left with an irreplaceable void in my life. It took a long time for gratitude to replace disbelief and grief. My father had been with me until I was deep into middle age. Not every child is so lucky.

About a year after Pop's death, I thought about what I wouldn't do to have just five more minutes with him. Like the grain of sand in an oyster, the idea grew in my mind that others might long for five more minutes of their own. Cultivated over several years by the encouragement of family and many friends, that idea became this book.

A call for submissions was placed and hundreds of people, from around the world, took precious time to share testaments of love for those they have lost. We chose fifty-seven stories for their breadth, quality, and diversity. Among the chosen are heartfelt descriptions of final moments, speculations on what happens once we leave our mortal state, as well as tales of other losses: depleted nature, divorce, and a misplaced journal that served as confidant. The stories comprising *Just a Little More Time* go beyond death and grief to celebrate love and life.

Each story is unique. But they are also profoundly human and will resonate with every reader. If you find this book as moving to read as it was to publish, it will have accomplished its purpose.

It may have been silly of me to hope my indomitable father might live forever. All the same, he lives forever in my heart. With every passing day, I find myself having something entirely new to say to him, so that my "five more minutes" is not just a final farewell. It's a lifelong conversation that unfolds and changes as I do, finding its echo in a man whose memory grows larger and richer the longer I live.

I hope this book inspires similar feelings in you, the reader. Take your five minutes now—and take them again and again. We never know what tomorrow will bring, but we can know what we'd like to say to those we hold dearest.

Just A Little More Time: that's all this book asks. It's a lot.

Dane Chapin

Lost and Found

Some beautiful paths can't be discovered without getting lost.

—Erol Ozan

In the Presence of Grief

BY CHAYA SILBERSTEIN

Grief clings to me like an old man to his cane and
I wonder about Harry, routinely gazing out the window
every morning until lunchtime. Now and then
he'd turn his face upward with a serene gaze and
exuberantly exclaim, "Sun."
I encountered him once in the hallway exiting the
    bathroom.
He leaned on his cane and said to me with wonderment in
    his eyes,
"I just realized, I'm surrounded by women."

Grief follows me home one day and nestles up
in the corner of the kitchen where I roll out dough for
a holiday I probably won't attend.
"You once had a world you belonged to," Grief says.
"Now, what do you have?"
And I don't quite know how to respond
because it feels as if I fell off the canvas of my quaint little
    town
and no glue in the world is strong enough to hold me.

Grief visits in a dream,
occupying the form of a man I once loved
who gave up his life in front of a speeding train.
He tells me that life is intricate and delicate with ups and
    downs.
"You are lucky to be alive," he says. "You can effect change.
I see so much every day that disturbs me but
without a body, there's nothing I can do."

Grief curls up with me at night and

I give her space to breathe.
She tells me it's okay
to be sad just as it's okay
to be joyful just as it's okay
to just be okay.

Grief hands me a photograph.
I tell her I see worms crawling through soil
and seeds tapping a ceiling they'll soon break.
She packs a suitcase and tells me she's off to visit Harry.
"I'll be back if you need me. Until then,
remove your heart from storage.
The silver polish is located under the sink."

The Secret Life Of Objects

BY TOTI O'BRIEN

It was hard for her to find jewelry I could wear. I don't recall when I noticed it, and I never understood why.

During childhood I was seldom adorned. I remember asking for a necklace once. I said I wished for corals. An aunt heard me and bought me a pendant with assorted bracelets, pale pink. My joy was unrelated to how the beads looked on me—I'm afraid I never wore them. Their decorative function wasn't yet clear. The point seemed to be keeping them, possibly, in a drawer. Maybe, thinking about them—that part I probably omitted.

I found my booty, years later, buried away with other memorabilia. It had lost all trace of color: corals die, I was told, when not worn. The discovery appalled me.

Mother had a cult of jewelry inherited from grandmother, then passed down to my sister. I witnessed her dress-up ceremonies for a decade or more. In the morning she went to work, she came back for lunch, then headed to work again... as it was customary for siesta-related reasons. Six days a week, changing twice every day, for she cared for elegance. Wearing after noon what she had on earlier was wrong. She wouldn't unless an emergency occurred. In such case she would be nervous, uneasy. At lunchtime Mother slipped out of her suit and wore casual clothes, further multiplying changing sessions. It was a pastime, and quite innocent. She didn't smoke, after all...

I unfailingly attended her dressing rituals, learning lots about beauty through constant exposure to its patient making. Sure, it was beauty as she intended it. Still, it's not the finished product that counts, but witnessing what building it takes. Looking, touching, then looking again, stepping back, coming close, thinking, pondering with attention and care, Mother built beauty all over herself twice daily. I'm not sure of her reasons. I cannot judge the sanity of what could have been a compulsion. But it doesn't matter.

The assortment of all needed elements implied myriads of

choices, with jewels being, literally, the coronation. They arrived when all had been carefully compounded, the right shade of rouge had been picked, the right scent dabbed on, all personal items transferred to the appropriate purse (matching shoes, belt, scarf, coat, umbrella, and gloves).

Only then the treasure chest—a drawer locked with a golden key—was pulled open. After fumbling with dark velvet-lined boxes, Mother slowly produced a gamut of pieces she lovingly juxtaposed, spreading them on the bed, trying them against her lapel, her cleavage, her sleeve. She commented out loud, and I listened, following step by step her aesthetic process.

Jewelry was the last flourish of her constantly renewed self-portrait. The authentication.

At fifteen I became a goldsmith apprentice. My training was cut short for logistical reasons, but I had learned enough. I repaired whatever broke in Mom's arsenal, extending the practice to friends and relatives. Yet personally I didn't wear much. Earrings, sometimes (Mom didn't). And a long, beaded chain, multicolored, fitting all of my dresses. The dead corals of my childhood might have sealed my heart, preventing further affections.

On occasion, Mom brought gifts of jewelry from her travels. One for me, one for sister. Sis picked first. She had inherited the tradition—the long stations in front of the bedroom mirror, torn between two pairs of ear-clips, one hazel, one chestnut. Which one matched her eye shadow? Did the gold of this pair fight the stripe of her pantsuit? Did the stripe call for silver instead? Just like Mom. I was given what sister left aside.

Mother's gifts also highlighted my life's significant steps—marriages, childbirths. Bulky, heavy items, inconsistent with my features, my size, my clothes. After my divorce I pawned them. The sum paid for a mattress I urgently needed.

But one piece, the most glamorous, disappeared on the very day I received it. Quite a pompous choker—large pearls cast in white gold. I sighed when I saw it, knowing how costly it was, and how useless. After storing the trophy I went for a swim. Summer thieves breezed by then, grabbing camera, laptop, credit card, and the choker...I was relieved.

Hurt, as well, more than I would have thought. Something had been disfigured somehow. Something already cracked came apart, due to an extraneous pull. The universe has a way to intrude in the script and read the next line, though it never was cast for the part. It just invites itself.

The theft made an impression on Mom. Though she didn't comment, her giving spurt briskly shrunk. Still, a few years later she bought me a watch-ring. I had one my husband had given me long before—a modernist piece from a museum shop. It worked well until the battery died and couldn't be replaced. Mother looked for another ring. She found a different version. While the former was angular, hers looked like a daisy with five rounded petals. I liked it and I wore it. Later, sister asked to see it, noticing the watch hands were invisible. Way too small—reading time was impossible. Therefore it was useless, she declared. As a matter of fact I agreed.

Mother must have overheard. I found her in a corner, her face buried in her hands. She was crying and she didn't dare look up. I immediately knew the cause of her tears: what sister and I had said. She had carefully looked for that ring.

She insists on passing down some of her belongings, before she dies. When I visited (oh so briefly) she reiterated her intention, then she sat with her golden-keyed drawer—the same—placed over her knees. Having finally realized my unfitness for necklaces, pins, bracelets, we concentrated on rings only. She displayed her collection, with long didactic detours. Some were set aside for my sister, who was asked first. But there were options left and I chose. Mom gave me the amber, the amethyst, a grained silver ball, and the lava stone that—she said—is worth a buck, but is my favorite. So far I have lost none.

Recently she presented me once more with a travel souvenir. The one sis didn't fancy: a brass ring with three minuscule stones. I was moved...it befitted me...was it the first time? I kissed mother, and I carefully put the gift away.

On the last day of my visit I looked in my purse, on my bed stand, everywhere, persuaded I had lost it. Mom reassured me, saying it wasn't worth much. But we both knew it wasn't the point.

I had sent my luggage ahead. I checked on arrival and there was the ring. I had only thought it was gone, torturing myself for a day with no reason. Maybe I needed such short-lived agony to get cleared, to cry something out.

Last month Mother travelled to her town of birth, to visit with relatives. Her hometown is famous for corals—they are found not far from the coast, mounted, then sold in place. En passant I mentioned it on the phone. I recalled the pink ornaments I had owned as a child. Suddenly I craved pink coral again. A tender, throbbing shade—it used to be my color. There weren't many things rosy when I grew up. It might be time to fix such imbalance.

Mom went souvenir shopping: pins for cousins, rings for aunts, I don't know what for sister, and a red necklace for me. Pink corals—she reported—weren't found anymore. But red! I'd never wear it. I choked with disappointment. I wished for no choker to keep in my closet, to be stolen, or pawned.

Given Mom's age and mine, should I take whatever she bought and shut up? Well, such wisdom was out of my reach. I told her I didn't wear red—or necklaces, by the way. I suggested someone else would enjoy the gift, and she followed my advice, seeming peaceful. I hope she didn't cry in a corner.

I did briefly. I was kind of dismayed. But the foolish pretense! Something I could actually wear, from Mom! A memento especially purchased for me, matching my wish.... Wait a second. Didn't I recently get one such gift? My brass ring? Wasn't it enough? Where was it, indeed? That is when I realized I had misplaced it again. When I wanted for more, I had lost what I already had.

Things' inability of speaking for themselves drives me crazy. The idea that lost objects are somewhere—perhaps very close— blows me away. When things aren't in view they still exist. They don't fly, do not vanish. They don't die, except for corals. They are hidden but, alas, remain quiet. Why don't they appeal to our sense of hearing? It would only be logical. Why don't things call?

I say this for keys, purses, wallets, eyeglasses, whatever "I can't find." Such words could be spared if selected items came with built-in devices—a birdcall, an alarm going off as soon as a given radium is trespassed. How I wished Mom's ring had one such.

Luckily its absence was brief. I was on the toilet when I found it. Why do I report such trivia? It's important. It's about the state of mind I was in, right then—necessarily humble. Believe me, I'm not being vulgar for the sake of it. When you sit on the toilet you don't have much of an attitude. You literally relinquish anything superfluous. You let go, and it works at more than one level.

Sitting on the toilet—half a second before getting up—the

resentful mood I had nursed for a day snapped off. I forgave Mom for picking the wrong gift—resulting, of course, in no gift at all. It wasn't her fault. On the contrary, she had tried, and that counted. And it wasn't my fault to be who I was—maybe difficult, maybe different.

On this one thought my gaze fell, inclined at the weirdest angle. Under my sewing table, stuck against wardrobe boxes, the ring peeked at me. I was transfixed. I would never have spotted it if not from that very place—door ajar, since no one was home at the moment. A blade of sunlight hit the stones, sneaking in the gap between the cloth and the floor.

I must have removed it while sewing, one day earlier—an unconscious gesture, promptly forgotten. It fell without me noticing, then it rolled away.

I'm so glad it made itself manifest after such a brief latency. I appreciate its will to remain in spite of my distraction, my carelessness. There's wisdom in such decision. I can sense it—the wisdom. I can smell it...what a late bloomer.

Wake-up Call

BY AUBREY MONTOYA

"Incoming call from Weber County Jail, Inmate Number 551. Do you accept charges?"

"Yes," I answer.

"Baby, can you please ask them to get me out of here, please?"

I can't stand the sound of her voice when she cries. It breaks my heart, and it shouldn't. She made the choice to do what she did, so I shouldn't have to pay for it. My heart shouldn't hurt for her, because hers never hurt for me. I'm in the middle of eating dinner, but I miss her, so I let her talk and make all of her usual promises.

"I'm going to change, I promise, Goose."

I love it when she calls me that. It reminds me of when I was a child, and everything was okay, even when it wasn't.

"Mom, you say you're going to change every time you almost ruin your life."

I hate being so hard on her, but sometimes I feel like that's the only way I can reach her. I can play with her emotions and I can hurt her feelings because it's my way of getting back at her for all the pain she has caused me.

I'm nine months pregnant and I don't want to have to deal with this anymore. I wish I never did have to deal with this. I wish we could pick our family; I would have chosen rich or maybe even educated parents. She causes most of the stress in my life.

– – –

It is Thursday night, and I wake up—not in my room. I'm kind of confused as to where I am but then remember that I'm just on the living room couch. I was there because my mom and dad were fighting and I wanted to make sure she went to bed safely.

I feel the need to go check on my mom. She's not in her room and she's not upstairs, either. So I check on my two-year-old twin brothers and my one-year-old sister. They are all in their cribs sleeping. *We are alone. No adult supervision, and I am only eight years old.*

I feel the familiar fear, sadness, and resignation. My mom always leaves us alone. I know where she is—she is out looking for my dad.

The house reeks with the scent of booze and marijuana. I open my brothers' and sister's bedroom door and leave my bedroom door wide open so that if they cry, I can hear them. I attempt to go back to sleep, but am terrified that something is going to happen.

The front door opens, and I hear my mom. She doesn't come upstairs to check on us, so I sneak across the hall, peek on my siblings, and close their door so that my mom will think we were all sleeping while she was gone. I sneak into my room because there isn't a blanket in the living room. Then I hear her scream, I hear my dad yelling at her, and I cover my head with a pillow. My body becomes tense and my stomach hurts because I know what's going to happen next.

She runs up the stairs. "Wake up! Help me get sissy ready. I'll get the boys!" She shrieks in pain.

I cry out, "Mommy, where are we going to go?"

"I don't know, baby, but we need to hurry."

We run out of the house and get into the puke-green van. We drive to a 7–Eleven. My mom tells me to recline my chair and fall asleep. But I can't. I'm scared for our safety. I lean to the side of the door, tears in my eyes.

I ask in a whisper, "Where are we going to live now, Mommy?"

"We're going to live at home. He's just drunk and can't think straight," she says confidently, a ring of purple around her left eye and dried blood around her nose.

- - -

"Incoming call from Weber County Jail, Inmate Number 551. Do you accept?"

"Yes."

"Can you come to my court date? It's next Tuesday."

"Mom, my doctor is inducing me next Wednesday." I can't take this anymore. She's driving me crazy, stressing me out to the point of no return.

"WHAT? You have to get me out of here, baby, please, please, baby. I have to be there for you. *I want to be there for you.*"

I can hear her voice crack, and I start to get choked up. I don't want to cry for her, I don't want to feel bad for her, but she is my mom, and her fifteen-year-old daughter is pregnant. She loves me no matter how bad I messed up, and I have to love her no matter how bad she messes up.

"Grandma and I will be there. Don't make me regret this."

"I love you, Baby Goose. Don't have baby Peanut without me."

I hang up the phone, wishing I wouldn't have hung up without telling her I loved her, too.

She had better change. PLEASE let her change.

- - -

I'm on the verge of a mental breakdown. I am so tired of my life and the way people treat me. I am so sick of people acting like I am nothing, like I mean nothing. I am tired of being judged for things I say and things I do. I'm tired of myself and tired of looking in the mirror every morning and hating what I see.

I want to throw up every time I have to go out. I hate eating because I feel so fat. I hate sleeping because they call me lazy. I hate being awake too long because they ask if I'm on drugs. They are all hypocrites.

They make me hate myself, yet they are supposed to be the ones who encourage me to love myself. When I write my suicide letter, I won't say I love you, because I don't have love for any of them.

I walk past the bottle of Xanax just sitting on my grandma's night stand. I hesitate for a second, then walk out of her room, zip down the stairs, and lock the front door. I walk back upstairs, into her room, and pick up the bottle. There are maybe ten to fifteen pills left.

I focus my eyes deeply on the pills I could swallow down with the vodka in the freezer. It could end my life so sweetly. I get the booze from the freezer, grab the pills, and sit on the bathroom floor. I'm banging my head on the counter, tears are rolling down my cheeks, and my heart is racing. My head hurts, my bones hurt. I smell the booze, smell the bottle of pills, but for some reason, I can't do it.

My mind races to the time my brothers called me, telling me they were in Boy Scouts, and that they were having so much fun doing all the things they loved; and the time my little sister spent the night at my house and got me up to do her hair for school; to the time I was a little girl and went with my grandparents for the summer to travel the country and explore new things— back when they loved me and enjoyed having me around. Now they can't wait to get rid of me. They hate me. They are more disappointed in me than ever. And then I jump back to reality, pop a pill in my mouth, close the bottle, take a swig of the vodka, close the bottle, put them back where I got them, and lay my head on my pillow.

I know that I'll wake up, back to my hell of a world, and I'll have to deal with this shitty thought for the rest of my life. I just want it to end, but I'll have to postpone it—at least for now.

— — —

"Incoming call from Weber County Jail, Inmate Number 551. Do you accept?"

"Yes."

"You're sure you're coming tomorrow, Goose? I really want to be there for you and the baby."

I feel a kick in my stomach. I'm not sure if it's my baby or my nerves.

"Yes, Mom. I'll be there."

— — —

The night of my inducement has finally arrived. We walk in, I get settled in my room, and a nurse begins running the cords and inserting an IV in my vein. She then leaves the room.

This is the moment I've been waiting for since the day I learned I was pregnant.

My boyfriend, Randy, walks his mom and little brother out. I call my grandma at home and tell her that she and Mom can come to the hospital. Things are getting intense. I'm tired and in a lot of pain. Finally my nurse comes in.

"Okay, are you ready for the epidural?"

"Yes, please."

My mom is standing at the door and asks if she can be in the room with me while they give me the epidural, but the nurse tells her that only the father can be in the room.

I place my feet on Randy's legs and he looks terrified, but I probably look just as scared. The anesthesiologist is placing the biggest needle I have ever seen into my back. *God, this is the worst pain I have ever felt in my life.*

After the epidural, my mom and grandma are allowed to stay with me awhile. Then they both leave to go to the waiting room. It doesn't bother me that my grandma isn't in the room with me, because I know she doesn't want me to be too overwhelmed with all the people that are in here. But I'm angry with my mom. She brought her boyfriend with her to the hospital, and I don't want him in my room. He's not my dad. He's not the grandfather. For Christ's sake, he's five years older than I am! I'm so irritated that she's outside with him and not in here with me. I convinced my uncooperative extended family to bail her out of jail so she could be here with me like she kept saying she wanted to be, but she's out there with him instead?

– – –

I'm exhausted. The morning rolls around and I decide to give up on sleep, because why sleep if I could have my son any time now?

"IT HURTS!" I screech in pain.

"We know, baby, you'll be okay," my mom says. She has finally sent her boyfriend home and has come back to my room.

Everybody is here. Randy claims his spot on my right, and my grandma is on the bench next to him, helping him help me. My aunt is rubbing my feet and my cousin is rubbing my back. I'm in tears because it burns. I feel nauseated.

I scan the room for my mom; she's on her phone next to my grandma. I want to be irritated, but I'm too focused on pushing this kid out.

I don't understand how someone who created me could be so uninvolved in my life, so distant from me, even though I went through hell trying to get her here. She promised me she would be here for me. Obviously that's not the case. I don't care anymore. I'm going to take my relationship with my mother and learn from it. I will never be distant from my son, I will know everything about him, and I will never leave his side. He will never grow up wondering where I am, because I will always be there.

The pain increases and I push until I think I can't push anymore. Until finally, the doctor has a head in her hands. And then a whole body.

He's finally here! I never thought that I'd love someone so much at first sight, but he is beautiful. He is the greatest thing to ever happen to me. He makes me so happy, and he's only been in this world for about 1.5 seconds.

— — —

It's a Friday night. I'm staring at my phone and I get a notification from my friend, Serenity, on SnapChat. She's at one of the biggest concerts of the summer.

A wave of sadness hits me. I wish I was there instead of here with the responsibilities of parenthood.

— — —

I glance back down at my phone. "Incoming call from Mom." I'm relieved that it's her voice and not that dreaded automated jail tone.

"Hi, Goose, how are you and the baby doing?"

Hearing her words snaps me out of my sadness. I look at X-Zavian, who is sleeping next to me, and I think about how happy I am to be here with him. I am no longer depressed and no longer feel like I don't belong in this world. Because now I have a purpose—my son is my purpose. I can't help but stare at him. I feel so loved. It's a love I haven't felt before.

"Hi, Mom. We're just hanging out. We're doing great."

Things Left Behind

BY JENNY CUTLER LOPEZ

Anxiety is hot nausea in my throat as I pack my school bag four days after high school graduation. A few T-shirts, jean-shorts, a hoodie, a hairbrush, a toothbrush, a couple of pens, a little red notebook, some money—maybe sixty dollars. My dad doesn't say much as he drops me and my boyfriend off at the highway, heading west. He leaves us in the cool morning air, the dew not yet evaporated from the never-ending east coast forest. We stick out our thumbs and within ten minutes we catch our first ride.

My boyfriend is an ugly wound. But he's a way out. In the past year, he's convinced me women are whores and no one loves me like he does. High school is a waste of time. He berates me if I correct him, like when I tell him Mexicans speak Spanish, not Mexican. Sometimes he plays the savior, but usually he's a black-haired troll. He smells like dirty laundry but I tell myself this is love.

Our first ride drives us eight-hundred miles straight to Ottawa, and by day two we are three-hundred miles farther west in Toronto. In our pup tent pitched close to the Trans-Canada Highway, I fall asleep reveling in the big city smog, weighed down by sticky heat, excited by this dirty, dangerous world. We hitchhike in jolts and bumps for an entire week through the fly-infested, northern reaches of Ontario. No food and red-hot arguments filling the dead silence of long days in rural wastelands.

I cannot confide in my boyfriend. Instead I confess my sins, craft angsty poetry, and celebrate small wins in the red, lined notebook tucked in my schoolbag. One of those sixty-nine-cent, flimsy notebooks you buy in a pharmacy. The red notebook hears all about our arrival in Calgary's suburban dust and about meeting my boyfriend's mother, a pot smoker who clips her frizzy hair with plastic flower barrettes. How my boyfriend begins to say, "It makes me sick just to look at you." How, in turn, I become ice cold. My lack of response makes him froth, driving him crazy enough to follow me around like an abandoned dog, until he forces me to have sex, sickening me.

I write about the tickle of roaches on my legs in the by-the-hour hotel in cop-prowling downtown Winnipeg. The hot rural breeze snaking through tall burnished crops and into my ear, convincing me the world whispers messages about futility and isolation and fate.

My notebook hears how gross it feels to not have any tissue for the unrelenting snot on my upper lip as my boyfriend screams, "Get the fuck out of here. No one wants you here." How I weep through my gut-rotting desperation my first night on a mildewed single mattress in a boarding house, which reeks of damp carpet and stale pee. I write about how I don't know how to break our bond when it feels like he's all I've got. I'm seventeen, and I pin my faith on an unfounded certainty I can cheat the heartbreak of loving a man who does not love me back.

I never leave my little red notebook in my new room. I'm afraid the dead-eyed boarders with whom I share the gas stove and stained bathroom, hardened men struggling to leave behind old habits, will steal it. I hide the notebook from my new coworkers at the coffee shop and in my staff locker at the movie theater.

In late August, my boyfriend and I walk into Kmart after watching a dollar-movie at the mall. On the bus back to the boarding house, I push my hand into my schoolbag and the familiar feel of paper thickened by use is not there. I know exactly where my red notebook sits—atop a stack of plates in the dining ware section of Kmart, where I rested it after writing.

I cross the road to take the next bus back to the mall. Metallic anxiety swells from my stomach to my throat and I feel as though I'm dreaming, unable to run, like I'm in thigh-high snow. I reach the plastic plates and bowls stacked on a display in the center of Kmart. It's not there.

"Did you see a red notebook here on these dishes in the last couple hours?" I ask a tall, bearded employee. I speak slowly to demonstrate my willingness for him to take time to think about it. He shakes his head without thinking. "Nope," he says.

I ask the manager wearing a cowboy hat about a lost-and-found. "You can leave your number," he says. I don't have a number. "Well, then check back tomorrow," he says.

I take the bus back the next day, but nothing.

That night, and the night after that, I lie in bed at the boarding house, unable to sleep. I wonder if someone picked up my little red notebook. I hope so. I hope he scanned the pages, stopping on a sentence. I hope there was a line where he connected with me even just for a moment before he threw it out with the rest of the trash.

Splitsville or Bust?

BY WENDY STALEY COLBERT

My husband, Mark, and I sat side-by-side in the oncology surgeon's office in Bellevue, Washington, listening to her describe the pros and cons of lumpectomy and radiation versus mastectomy and reconstruction. To the doctor, we looked like a united, if not happy, forty-something couple. After the cancer diagnosis, she wouldn't expect smiles. She would not have known that I rarely sat this close to Mark anymore or that over the past year I'd bought black, lacy underwear as an attempt to reclaim the role of Mark's lover. She probably thought the worried expression on my face was due to the thought of surgery and not about the equal concern that this diagnosis placed me back in un-fun, un-sexy wife territory.

The surgeon handed me a slip of paper filled with charts and statistics that reminded me of the microbiology research my father used to carry in his briefcase. I grasped the sheet and read through every word, looking up once in a while to nod at the doctor, then passed the sheet to Mark. He glanced at the page and set it down on the desk in front of me. Then the doctor pulled a binder from the shelf, flipped it open on the desk, and slid it toward me.

"Dr. Wells does great work," she said, pointing to a photograph.

A page protector covered the picture of a headless woman's bare chest. I turned the page, and there on the other side was the plastic surgeon's business card.

Dragging the binder closer, I turned back to the photo and leaned over it. How strange to not only be directed to look at breasts, but also be granted license to stare. The only other pictures of breasts I'd studied were in *National Geographic* and in a few of Mark's old *Playboys*. I'd hardly seen my mother's or friends' breasts naked, and in those rare instances I'd only allowed myself a polite, passing gander. I remembered as a child being surprised when my mother took off her padded bra and her real breasts hung down, no longer conforming to the rounded, uplifted mold

I was used to seeing under her turtlenecks. Now my curiosity was allowed full rein and I gazed at the photo in the binder, wondering how Mark's twenty-four-year-old lover Erika's breasts compared. "They're beautiful," I said. Full, circular, voluptuous, not saggy. "The nipples look real."

Having nice-sized, perky, artificial breasts wouldn't be so bad. I could surgically adopt ancient symbols of youth, health, and fertility. But the decision wasn't purely about cosmetics.

"How do they feel?"

The doctor said something about loss of sensation, that without tissue and one's own nerves, the breasts are numb. "Sometimes a little feeling on the surface returns," she said.

What did that mean? Were the breasts numb the way my mouth was after getting wisdom teeth pulled? Except the numbness never wore off? I didn't ask. I was willing to sacrifice my pleasure for better odds of future health. If the woman in the photo was standing here naked in front of me, I could ask her if her new breasts pleased her and how they felt. I could examine her breasts in real time and touch them, maybe even watch as Mark ogled and fondled them. I'd rather he touched these breasts than Erika's. I slid the binder sideways over the desk for Mark to see.

"It's up to you," he said.

The doctor gave me a folder full of information and then walked us out to the nurse, who collected some of my spit. She'd mail the sample off to a research company to see if I had a mutation on one of the breast cancer genes. Women who had these mutations had a much higher risk of getting both breast and ovarian cancer and having them recur.

Walking out to the car, I clutched the folder. Mark said, "I'll love you with or without breasts." He was doing and saying the right things—sitting by my side at appointments, expressing his supposed commitment. But his words and his actions didn't comfort me. By that time, our love had become double-edged—equal parts care and abandonment. We could hardly stand to be in the same room together, our bodies concrete reminders of how together we'd failed.

As soon as we got back to the house, we went to separate corners—Mark walked into the home theater to watch a movie and I walked into the office, sat down at the desk, grabbed a spiral notebook and pen, and started making phone calls.

First I dialed the other side of the country to talk to one of my best friend's sisters, who'd had a double mastectomy and breast reconstruction a couple of years earlier, even without any trace of malignancy. JoJo had watched her mother die of breast cancer and wanted to remove any possibility of that fate from her own future. I'd met JoJo, a sassy redhead, when we were in our early twenties, and she knew my personality, so I trusted her opinion when she said, "Double mastectomy, reconstruction, it's not that bad, Wendy. You can do it."

I put a checkmark next to JoJo's name and number. She was right. I could lose part of myself and pretend I hadn't.

A boom sounded from the walled-off theater where Mark sat, making my chest vibrate.

The next call was to a plastic surgeon.

When I walked into that first plastic surgeon's office some days later, I brought my list of questions: Did she prefer working on patients with single or bilateral mastectomies? Was reconstruction possible after radiation? Where did the tissue for the new nipple come from?

A nurse handed me a binder, not unlike the one Mark and I had seen in my own doctor's office, and told me to check out this doctor's work.

I opened the binder and there on my lap lay the naked, headless torso of another anonymous middle-aged woman with folds of skin on her upper belly, below her mastectomy scars. Next to her "before" picture was her "after" picture, the same torso months later with the striking addition of rounded globes, simulated breasts. Pretty good. I bet Mark would like these. Closing my eyes, I pictured the globes on my chest, then a man's hands caressing them. Why couldn't I picture his face? Was he Mark or some other man?

As I leafed through the photos in the binder, my eyes misted over. I could see why these women were called survivors. In the pre-reconstruction photos, the women looked like they'd lived through a battle, as if a sword had smitten off their tits. These women seemed somehow stronger than war veterans, though. I didn't put myself in the same class as these women in the binder. They probably survived late-stage cancer, radiation, chemotherapy, the works—not stage zero, like me. My case seemed wimpy by comparison. The strongest women in my mind were those who chose not to reconstruct. Those who accepted their changed bodies, as is. But that wasn't me.

What would the male equivalent be? Ball removal? How many men would be willing to do that? Would Mark? Was scrotum reconstruction even a viable surgery? If a surgeon could give a man bigger cojones, would he do it? Maybe.

Every once in a while a photo in the binder was of a single-breasted woman, someone like my mother and me, who must've had cancer on only one side. Mom had kept both her breasts. Was that to please herself, or my father? It was too private a question. I'd never ask; I'd never know the answer. Had my mother sacrificed her future health by keeping both breasts? A one-breast reconstruction ended up lopsided. The pictures proved it. The nipples didn't perfectly line up; the color of the areolas was a shade or two different; one nipple stood permanently erect, the other flat; the fake breast was a little higher and rounder than the droopier natural breast. I knew that if a woman gained or lost weight, her real breast did, too, while the artificial breast remained static. But the woman who kept the healthy breast kept all of that sensation. Sensation I'd been tamping down lately. Keeping a little distance from myself had come to feel normal.

Later that week, I met with another doctor, who told me what radiation would be like if I went that route. Then, I met with three more plastic surgeons to hear their recommendations. I gathered and analyzed all of these findings as if I were a mathematician or a scientist like my dad. Even in this most womanly of decisions, my father was the model. I was coming to my decision in the same way I thought my father would if he were in my place.

Could I love my new breasts as my own? Or would I view them as something the doctor had created, separate from me? If I kept one breast, could I live with the risk of getting uterine cancer by dutifully swallowing a Tamoxifen pill daily for five years? Would I worry every year when I went in for my one-sided mammogram?

Days later, the oncology surgeon's nurse called me with the BRCA test results. I had a non-standard mutation on the BRCA2 gene. She couldn't tell me what my odds of recurrence were. I penciled down this information and hung up.

The test findings were inconclusive. I'd have to make my own decision.

Similar to how I felt about my marriage.

I decided to have a bilateral mastectomy and then breast

reconstruction. Mastectomy would give me less than one percent chance of recurrence on the chest wall and the best cosmetic results, since the reconstruction surgeons could design the new breasts at the same time, using the same materials to match. I wouldn't need to take Tamoxifen. I wouldn't have to expose myself to the radiation of mammograms, since I'd never need one again. I wanted her to remove my nipples, too, since the cancer had started so close to that area, and I didn't want to risk saving any tissue where the cancer had been. I was choosing the mastectomy to give me as much future good health and as much peace of mind as possible. I was choosing reconstruction for the looks.

"All right. I can tell you've done your research." The doctor paused for a beat and looked at Mark, then back to me.

"You realize your sex life won't be the same. Other patients have told me they wish they would've known."

I glanced at Mark and looked back at the doctor, nodding and thinking, sure, it'll change. Breast-less sex meant working harder to prove to myself I was desirable while feeling more numb than I'd been since I found out he'd cheated.

Regardless of changes to my sex life, this I knew for sure: My breasts and I were breaking up. I'd lose my curves and the feeling in my chest, and I'd recover what shape and sensation I could. I'd develop a healthy relationship again. If not with Mark, then with a new man. But first with my new body, then my new bust.

Still Life

BY TERRY SEVERHILL

Thin,
Tall,
Clear,
Light green glass vase
Stems thornless
Petals randomly carpet the table top
The apple in the basket
Formerly green
Now a worrisome yellow
Forgotten banana
Mostly brown
The white-haired gentleman
Sits
Next to the table
Next to the window
Retired
The kids long since moved
Too far away
Now widowed
Still life.

Paying to Sleep Alone

BY LAURA HART

I am a comfort sleeper. That's not a description of the self—it's what I do. That's my occupation. I sleep around.

In the most literal sense of the meaning, not to get lost in the risqué euphemism the expression has become. Those who respond to my ads do so to feel a physical presence beside them as their eyelids droop closed amongst the current of sheets. We are here. Together.

We do not touch or speak. We do not tangle our limbs together as goose bumps step into our heartbeat. No one hushes or caresses or coos away tears. We do not share stories of our families or the last time we smiled. Or the last time we made someone else smile. He does not brush the hair from tickling my cheek. She does not press herself against my back, one hand on my shoulder as a reminder she is there. We do not lie awake in the night, pretending the other person smells like he used to or breathes like she would, or tasting the air for anything that might quench our nostalgia.

Unless we do.

I've learned that it takes at least three to five years in a role before you're no longer considered entry level. I guess that makes me an expert. A bona fide dream catcher. A painter of the art of sleeping. My ads shine like teardrops, awkward and dripping through Craigslist—posted only for those confused enough to understand my services. Targeting humans so deeply grounded in loneliness that blushing is no longer an issue as they reach out to touch a stranger. All of our limbs will quickly fall asleep together, numb and prickling hot with needles as we try to force ourselves to breathe deeper than we have been. To experience the past through jagged imaginations grown cold and uncreative from years left unstimulated.

The first to find me was Meryl. Her nose was slender and

perfect unless looked at from the side, where it pointed out like a compass confused about which way was north. The thinness of her pitch-dyed hair, roots dusted in gray, suggested she was late fifty-something going on senile. Meryl cried as the weight of the darkness pushed down upon our chins, casting moonbeams upward to catch on the branches of our eyelashes.

"How did you get into this business, dear?"

I was not accustomed to the first words a person spoke to me to be phrased as a question. Her vision did not turn to cast upon my cheek. Her eyes remained closed as she clutched a rosary worn thin from the oils of handprints.

"Being alone," my words stung like a toothache, deep and without origin, "for too long."

"Have you always been alone?"

"No and I suppose that's the problem. If I hadn't been a part of someone else, perhaps I never would have known that I was aching."

"You're lucky." She must have heard my tongue catch behind my teeth because she hurried to finish. "If you're lonely because you love someone now who doesn't love you back, that's not something to worry about. It just means someday you will come to love someone else. It's the people who are lonely because they don't love anyone who need to worry."

I turned to face the horizon, which began to flush pink to welcome the rising sun. Meryl's body became still as my eyelids reached each other. My hands stretched out, inquiring to be held. I clasped them together to remind them being held is not what we were there for.

Rodger's bedroom was tucked away in camouflage. That was the fourteenth bed I would sleep in the first year. The air hung stale like smoke clouds around our sticky bodies. We were kept company by a stuffed deer, whose corneas upon death had been replaced with dollar-store googly eyes.

"That there is Buck," Rodger grunted. His rough hands pulled at his beard, massaging the knotted burgundy. His breath stuttered heavy and methodical, each inhale visibly draining him. His knuckles were the size of my cheekbones as they lay heavy on the pillow beside my face.

"Mmm," I replied. Canisters of chewing tobacco lined his

only dresser, resting haphazardly in a forgotten pile. Along the windowsill stood skeletons of plants that had long ago surpassed their life, though the artistically designed pots suggested that once upon a time they had been loved.

"It hasn't always been like this, ya know." He choked out a mottled *heh* as if to make light of a situation I was judging him for. They all did this. Made excuses for hiring someone to sleep beside. Rushed explanations drafted out of their pressure points like overly applied cologne.

"Mmm."

They all forgot that I was here too. No one considered that, maybe, I was a comfort sleeper because I needed the comfort too. No one considered that everyone who sleeps by themselves at night gets lonely sometimes. Lonely people only see themselves as alone.

Rarely did I meet someone who avoided talking about their job, if they were going to speak at all. Even more rarely did I find someone with a more bizarre profession than my own. Four and a half years in, though, I finally did.

Rita was a professional apology writer. She had olive skin; dark eyes that contained a peppering of green; and long, fake fingernails. She texted on her phone more than we spoke, her nails against plastic erupting like the pattering of rain. The companies she worked for had some bad publicity, she explained.

"So, people bring me on to apologize for it." Shrugging, Rita continued tap-dancing on the touch screen of her phone. "Like, to the world in general, though. Someone writes a bad review, I draft and send out an apology."

Rita had a way of speaking like most chew bubble gum. The thoughts came out slowly, she took a while to process in-between, but then words burst from her mouth and ended on a high note.

"We at our organization," she recited robotically, "apologize for any inconvenience we may have caused. We do strive to provide a professional, comfortable, and efficient work place, and apologize we could not meet your standards." A laugh pauses her speech and she rolls her eyes, processing her next words. "While we make an honest attempt to respond to all emails, questions, and concerns in a timely manner, things do get busy from time to time, and we hope you understand."

Her arm reaches towards mine, beckoning me to listen closely.

"Ready? Because this is the real kicker." She sucks in a big breath and closes, "We offer you our most sincere apologies and wish you all the best."

"That's good," I say, deeply understanding the need for a good apology.

"The real joke is I *copyrighted* that." Her fingers pause to concentrate on what she is about to tell me. "Those words in that order belong to me, and companies hire me every day to send the lines out somewhere."

"I wonder how an apology can be sincere if it's purchased."

"Well, that," one finger raises from the phone to point dramatically upward, "is not my problem."

I guess when it's not your problem, there is no need to apologize. Unless, I suppose, the problem was inadvertently caused by you. A string-theory of small but unrelated instances, or maybe just wishing too hard, for too long.

I kept the last roses that my husband would ever give me. That was six years ago. I laid them out across my vanity; there was something strikingly beautiful about the death of a beautiful thing. The last glimpse of life amongst dried-up petals, or the purpled-paper of eyelids.

Danny was the youngest of everyone I had slept with. Or next to. I had to remind myself that I was no longer privy to the wording nor the action that implied physical contact. Danny kept one bare arm linked underneath my own. His touch was smooth as the breeze streaming through the open window that turned our skin to butter. I hummed along to the tune of the night sky while his silky curtains pirouetted in rhythm. The blueness of Danny's veins were accented by the burn marks where needles had pierced his flesh. His naked skin lay bald and exposed. He could not furrow a brow or bat a lash; he could not massage a beard or dye his roots. He told me it felt like fire, as a hanging bag emptied throughout his organs.

"When it's done, though," the corners of his lips twitched in an echo of satisfaction, "everything feels so wonderful. There is no greater pleasure than the removal of a consistent ache."

"I heard that afterward it makes you sick." I caught myself weighing in on things I do not know about. "I thought, anyway."

Next to his bed there was a picture of a healthier him: a Danny with hair and a genuine smile. His arm lay around the waist of a slender brunette, dressed in crimson, holding a single orange flower. The saffron petals pushed tightly against her blazing dress. I assumed Danny felt her absence like spices on the tip of a tongue.

"Oh, I meant life." He found confusion in my stare and added, "Just in general."

When Danny slept, his face looked like it had been drawn on with wet ink, the milky paper of his cheeks swimming around the purple crescent of his mouth. I closed my eyes and begged for Danny—or maybe myself—to morph into someone else. Someone with skin the color that skin should be, and eyes that could still smile, a mind that could rest at night, and an infinitely stretching set of years to want to live for.

Gifts of Love

One word frees us of all the weight
and pain of life—that word is love.

—Sophocles

Woman at the Well

BY KIM BEYER, MA

I rest my ear on the beating heart of literature daily, my eyes closed, my hands folded in my lap. For all my scholarly background, I know Biblical literature is more than history, sociology, or law. I read for an intuitive meaning—for the wisdom of those who have lost so much and yet rise with each day. Usually, I respond to my experiences with poetry, the language that almost breaks free of rules and assumptions and artificial boundaries. Today, I respond in prose. Walk with me now, and meet the Lady at the Well...

I shadow her as she lays another cloth on his head, this man-cousin of hers, who has been ill for months. Only in her earliest thirties, her dusky face is riddled with fine wrinkles, her black hair shot through with wiry strands of gray. Her breath is light and even, as if impending death is no stranger to her home. I move around her simple, one-room house, the unseen spirit from a far future, touching this old sword, that fold of men's clothing. They are all kept like funeral urns, reminders of the life that once filled such things. I can smell the illness here, and when she reaches for the water jug, I know it is as much a time of relief from her vigil as it is a need for any water.

In my mind, I trail her down to the well, smiling in wonder at her sure gait, the way she shoulders a pot I would struggle to hold with both hands even if it were empty. The heat folds and shimmers around us, so dry that my nose pinches tight and the edges of my lips crinkle. I know a man will come to the well soon, the man we call Jesus, and he will enter into a conversation with her that has echoed down through the ages.

But I wonder, my feet falling into the dusty outline of her footprints, what assumptions we make about her from our translation of a translation of a third-hand remembered event in the Bible. Five husbands, we are taught, but I could see their echoes in her tiny abode—these were not divorces but losses, five men in a row taken by plague or war or accident or too much drink. How time devours the poor and how easily we, in our comfortable settings, forget. And the man in her home is far from a lover, despite what so many pastors claim today—he is a relation in her care alone, dying in the intimate way of two thousand and more years ago.

The sun cuts my eyes and I glance away. A woman at the well at noon—"she must be mad," later readers will claim. Surely that or she is difficult or avoiding the other members of the village. But I can smell the clean heat here, and the spaciousness of a chore done in quiet and care. There is an ancient tightness around her lips—holding back what she must not say, white teeth grinding on loss, on captivity, on the bondage of a fine mind to a deep and abiding poverty. I hear the voice she wants to use but feels she cannot.

This is how loss feels—we feel as if we stand alone.

I did not come to ask my own questions of her, but to simply see her as she is before the famous give and take with this Jesus, this Jewish Rabbi. I wanted only to see *the woman* as she sets the jug down and shields her gaze with the edge of her hand so she can better assess the stranger sitting there, well-side, waiting. Their eyes meet and there, with that searching glance, is where I smile at last.

Because if you know loss, then you know the way to speak with another. Not through platitudes or fixing, but through the glance, the touch of the hand to hand. Loss makes our skin very thin, our ears tremble so that even the breath can seem harsh. No, we understand how it is to yearn for *presence*—for someone to stand with us and see us in all our vulnerability and not turn away from the raw emotions.

And that is how they spoke, these characters in my imagination—heart began to talk to heart before a word was even spoken—not man to woman, nor Jew to Samaritan, not law to law or tradition to tradition. And when the verbal conversation began, he spoke truth without condemnation, reality without trying to fix any of it. But, more, he met her eye, nodded with her comments, took water from her hand and quietly challenged her to reach within herself for the place that never runs dry of life...

I let the two fade away, opening my eyes to my journal. For a long time, no words come. And then, at last only a soft sigh.

And for today, it is enough.

If Only

BY LORAINE WOLFF

We knew that you would die first. We joked that it could go either way, but with a twenty-three-year age difference, it was unlikely.

You could find humor in everything. You told me, "I've done everything I've wanted to in this life, and some things I probably shouldn't have. It's been a good life, and I am curious about what comes next."

As the end was upon us, symptoms were obvious. We joked the warranty was expired on your body. The pain became constant and you claimed, "This just isn't fun anymore."

We brought you home where you wanted to be, for even a few hours in a medical environment were torturous.

In your final week we talked of the end.

Me: So, honey, you're sure you are ready to die?

You: Yep, yesterday.

Me: You're sure? You just want to stay here at home?

You: Yep. I've done everything I've wanted to in this life, more than most people. The only thing I am worried about is you.

Me: Well, don't worry about me. You married a tough old broad. I'll be fine.

You: No, you won't...but then you will.

Me: OK. If you are really sure you want to die at home, that's up to you. [Then grinning.] But please don't make a mess.

During those last few weeks, I noticed how much more often

you thanked me for taking such good care of you. I wasn't
going out of my way. I was only doing what I have always
done: look for ways to make you happy, just like you did for
me.

IF ONLY...

If I could do anything with you again, it would be nothing.

You told me over and over again to slow down. You told me I
　　didn't need to be 'doing stuff' all the time. "It's important to
　　take time to contemplate your navel." I wondered how you
　　could sit so long doing nothing.

But now I wish I could sit on the deck and look at the water
　　and watch the ducks and herons and the weather changing
　　with you. I wouldn't fuss or bustle; instead I would savor
　　and absorb into my essence the joy and tranquility I felt
　　from you in those moments while sitting next to you.
　　I would hold your hand while appreciating all that we have.

William

BY DR. KAREN BREECK

It took three days before my brain thought to put "pregnancy" into my differential diagnosis. Having never been pregnant before, it wasn't a set of symptoms I initially recognized. I still remember the twinkle in the cashier's eyes and her once-over assessment of me as I purchased a pharmacy pregnancy test. I wondered if she thought I already had that special "glow." I still have that positive-sign test strip. My little piece of concrete proof that this was all really happening. I was going to be a mom.

As the weeks moved into months, the pregnancy and thoughts of becoming a mother became more and more real. Hearing the heart beat for the first time was exhilarating. Seeing him/her on the ultrasound and printing off his/her first "photo" was extraordinary. But nothing prepared me for the first kick. It was then, only then, that I really understood that there truly was something inside me that was me, and yet not me.

We picked his/her names—Katy for a girl, William for boy. I talked to him/her nonstop day and night—out loud and silently. We planned our new roles and relationships. We planned our new life together.

I must admit, I was scared. I was almost forty. As a first-time mother at my age, so much could still go wrong. Breathe in. Breathe out. Trust in the universe.

I was living alone—my military husband deployed to the other side of the world, Korea, and I also military, deployed to an isolated northern Canadian base. Work kept us both busy until we could be together again soon. Busy, busy, busy—so much to be done at work but also in preparation of a move to a new city for the baby and maternity leave.

Around my sixth month I just knew something wasn't right. I asked the local doctor to re-examine the baby by ultrasound. "Yes, he/she is still kicking and very active, yes...but something isn't right. I just know it," I told my doctor.

And...something wasn't right. The ultrasound wasn't showing

the landmarks expected at this stage of my pregnancy. I was sent away from my small base to see a big city doctor.

I arrived at the high-risk pregnancy unit at the same hospital where I trained during medical school ten years earlier, finding so much familiar, finding comfort in that familiarity.

First came the repeat ultrasound. I remember the happy and cheerful initial greeting of the ultrasound technician. Then as the ultrasound started, the smile soon faded. It was to be followed by the words no future parent ever wants to hear: "I'm sorry." "There are anomalies." "Not compatible with life." "Likely Trisomy 18."

Meanwhile, throughout that conversation, there was my son (yes, we knew now it was a boy!), kicking hard, kicking strong, and very much alive inside of me. There would be more tests. More problems found. And then the final determination... That at best... "Maybe he can live for a few days... Not more."

My husband was called to my side from Korea. He arrived the day before we decided to baptize him while still unborn, not knowing the outcome of the labor to come. Thirteen hours later, a beautiful baby boy was born. I held him. I rocked him. I talked to him. I told him all the promises and dreams and aspirations I had for him and me, together. He was beautiful. The nurse put a beautiful, baby blue, hand-knit hat on him and wrapped him in a white, angelic, crocheted blanket—gifts from other women who had gone through this before me—helping make William look even more perfect in his own imperfect way.

I still think of the women who knit those hats and blankets especially for times like these. The short time, when a mother holds her baby, her child, her flesh and blood, for the first and last time simultaneously. Having to say your goodbyes before you have had a chance to say hello is something no mother should ever have to do.

But I will always remember William forever in his hat and blanket. I know I wasn't the first, nor the last, to feel that pain of that day. Through their thoughts and crafts, I felt the love and sharing of my pain as if they were there with me, supporting me as I handed my baby over to the nurses for the last time.

The Non-Linear Nature of Loss

BY ANN TEPLICK

Even though you lose the rugelach—the recipe of cinnamon,
flour, cream cheese and plum—the kosher instructions
scribbled in Yiddish on scraps that have tanned into the
amber of your Lithuanian Nana

and even though you lose your wind vane—the rooster with
the copper headdress, cougar with the copper claws, the
upswing of the copper springbok

even though you lose the days when A leads to B to C to D, with
clarity, no ink spot of complacency, you lose your sense of
right and wrong, your compass gone

and even though you lose your jester—monk's cowl, mock
scepter, three-pointed hat that any fool would pole jump to
jingle its bells, you've back-flipped into the well, you lose
your sense of timing,

lose the memory of the time when the three of you swan dived
and one survived, when the collie died in the fire, when your
mother pushed you away while she was dying,

and you lose your virginity, over and over, lose your dignity, lose
the mask that plumps your cheeks, lusters your teeth, glue
peeled from the illusion that everything's okay, because you
lose your sense of self to reinvent and lose again the blues,
Mikado, gingerline,

you leave the bed, align your spine into a triangle to stable its
base, to brace for the ocelot that climbs from the basement,
and even though you lose the meter to your breathing,
stagger for your footing, your Nana waits with a mixing
bowl, glass, like a pasture of buttercups that bubbles with
rugelach, takes your doughy face into her hands, and speaks
in Yiddish, then, in English,

"My love, you will survive."

Choices

BY DANE CHAPIN

When don't I think about you, Pop? Maybe when I sleep? Even then you appear in my dreams, all the time. Sometimes those dreams are so real, I think you've somehow returned to earth, at least the earth I'm currently inhabiting. You didn't raise us in a religious household, so I'm not sure what happens when our time is up. Hopefully you do and are now smiling down on what I've become and am becoming.

A lot has happened since you made your departure, basically all good. There you are again. Optimism. Yes, you were the eternal optimist and the apple didn't fall far from the tree, fortunately, thankfully. "If it is not good at the moment, it will be," is a motto I live by. Your life and legacy continue on, not only in my heart but in my actions too.

In random discussions I have at times, I share my strongly felt sentiment that the best way to raise a child is by example. Pop, you were truly the perfect example. I often share with my own daughter the profound impact voluntary choice has in our lives. And how, going forward in life, choices would be hers to make, own, and live with.

I didn't have a choice in my enormously good fortune of having you as a father, role model, and mentor. I did have a choice in having you as a friend, my best, and having you as a business partner, the best. I can say, unequivocally, those were the best choices I ever made.

The choice I'd like to make now, more than anything in life, would be to have you back for five minutes, five days, five years, five decades. While that choice doesn't seem possible (I'll keep wishing), I do make the choice to honor you by trying to live an examined life that aims to give more than receive, just like you.

Give me these moments back...

BY MEGHAN SKYE

I sat on the edge of a bed I hadn't slept in for many years. In the heat of the summer night, the sheets were in a tangle and largely pushed aside. Leslie was wrapped around me, her leg bent over my hip, her head on my shoulder. I couldn't resist and ran my fingers through her hair. I felt a tightness in my chest—I'd never touch that softness again.

I shook my shoulder. "Meghan, wake up, I'm from a future. I only have a few minutes. This isn't a dream, listen. There's something I want you to understand. Pay Attention and Remember. I'm going to tell you something about love—live by it.

"Express love at every opportunity. This may be difficult at first, but as time passes it will become easier; more and more people will recognize this truth. Love is an intention and broad in definition. With harm to none, let your intention be loving and you will find love everywhere: a kind word, a reassurance, a smile, a hug... I'm not saying you'll never have a hard day, but that's where your investment will pay. On a trying day someone may say they value your friendship, give a hug at just the right time, or a stranger may smile and encourage you to laugh. Catching on?

"Love is an unlimited resource; the only way to deplete it is to fail to give it freely, openly, and authentically. Love has been abused, which is why authenticity is so important. You may perceive others as gaming or careless. If one cares less, it means less, they risk less, imagine they fear less. What is meaningless love?

"You never know when the last *anything* may be." I looked at Leslie. "So fix your intention to every moment, as if there will be no other. How do you want to remember it? What you withhold may haunt you.

"How do you want to remember her? Ravishing her, because her blouse fell open just so, or you'd rather have read a book? Give of yourself with utter delight and without reservation. Make love like it's the first, and the very last time, every time.

Complacency... Don't, just don't.

"There is true magnificence in her love. You have experienced the profound and know it for what it is, but you won't be able to comprehend its full meaning until it is gone. When you feel the pain is unbearable, remember the truths you learned, the gifts you received, and you will know the grace of divine freedom.

"Live this path and we may not meet again; this is a turning point. I love you. Now, sleep and remember."

I unfroze time and stepped outside of it again. I felt strange, dizzy, and then...filled with light.

I Do Not Know Your Name

BY KATHLEEN LAFRANCIS EATON, PH.D., (BUTTERFLY)

There are two words I must say.

Thank you.

After sixty years, I don't know where you are, or even if you are alive. But your bright brown eyes, framed with dark curls, and your big smile are still crystal clear in my mind. You smelled like fresh baked cookies. I breathed it in when you picked me up.

It was you that rushed me to the emergency room when the preacher's kid landed a rock on my head. I was blinded by blood. Was I going to be blind forever? You hugged me tight, though I screamed at every stitch. By the time my mother arrived it was over. She returned to work. You took me home.

During the time you were at our house, I got to be a child. For that I love you. My parents hired you to care for my siblings and me, to clean house, and cook. We weren't rich; my mother had to work. I learned later that in The South blacks didn't get paid much. And you had your own children to feed and care for.

What you did for me wasn't part of your job. If my parents had known, they would have fired you. In fact, no one would have ever hired you again. You witnessed unbelievable things that should never happen to anyone—especially to a child. I don't think I would have had the courage you did. Because it was the right thing to do, you found a way to stay, even at your own peril.

I told you they were crazy. You agreed. It gave me comfort to know that my thoughts were valid and normal; theirs were not. It was you who taught me that I could choose. I could choose not to be like them. I could be like you instead.

You spoke softly because you heard the violent screaming and saw me bounce off the wall when he found me hiding. He always found me fast, before Mommy got home. Mommy would never help. Ever. What could you do? There was no Child Protective Services. Psychologists didn't believe sexual abuse existed until the 1990s. Why would they believe you? No one ever believed me. Except you.

Thank you for staying and always comforting me after. That's more than some children get. When you went home at night, I got scared. You taught me how to comfort myself. You told me about fairies and how they were looking over me. "They will listen to you."

I sat out back talking to them. And they were real. For decades I held fairies in my memory, in my heart. Kids have imaginary friends. But mine were real! Go ahead, laugh! They were actually fireflies, beautiful fireflies.

Recently I held a butterfly drying its wings before its first flight. The heat of my hand gave it the warmth to dry its wings and fly. So beautiful!

You were the warmth I needed to survive. And because of you, I can now fly!

Mickey and Me

BY SUZY BLOUGH

Michael "Mickey" Gruber
(April 23, 1935–March 4, 2007)

Although I had ten days with you before you died, I never really got to say goodbye. Oh, I spoke to you daily, told you how much I loved you, what you meant to me, how much I'd miss you, and that I couldn't bear to see you go. But you were already in a coma by the time I got to the hospital. And while I sensed that you knew I was there, I never got to hear your effortless laugh, comforting words, and often unsolicited but always appreciated advice again.

When you died, I was really lost—especially when I returned to my life in Atlanta after sitting shivah with the family in Baltimore for a week following your funeral. I had been away for close to one month, and even though it was heart-wrenching and traumatic to watch you die, the ten incredibly nurturing days I had with Randi, Rich, and Mommy while visiting you in the hospital made it bearable. Likewise, the cocoon that shivah, friends, and family created protected me from the raw vulnerability and pain I felt.

When shivah ended, I had to return to being a mom, a wife, and an employee, responsible for everyone else's needs, with no room available for my grief. Each time I felt sad and lost, I'd pick up the phone to call you because no one else listened as well or championed me the way that you did. I'd dial your number and halfway through would realize *you're* the reason why I was feeling that way—and I would never be able to hear your voice and words of comfort again.

But as seven years have passed since your passing, I've discovered that's not quite true. Though physically you are no more—I still hear your laughter, see your sweet gap-toothed smile and the sparkle in your multi-hued blue eyes, and feel your unbridled love and support.

Mommy always said that of the three kids, I was most like you. While Randi and Richard each possess their share of "Mickey" attributes, I was the child who befriended and talked to anyone in my path. Like you, I am optimistic to a fault.

But perhaps one of the greatest gifts you gave me, which I only discovered in the past few years, is that I'm not afraid to reach out to people who are terminally ill. I assumed everyone felt this way, but while my dear friend Brian was dying from a brain tumor I spoke with him often, and he frequently mentioned that I was one of the few friends who still called him regularly, could honestly talk to him, make him laugh, and that I wasn't afraid of his response to the question of "How are you, *really?*" When he was only days from dying, I was honored to be invited to spend time with him and his family to help them through this tragic transition.

If a friend of yours was ill, especially one diagnosed as terminal, you would spend countless hours with him—talking, making him laugh, comforting, and lending a hand to the family in any way that you could. I never knew this, and, while not surprised, I'm intrigued by this newly discovered connection to you. And by being able to do the same with my loved ones, I know that who I am and who I am becoming are your gifts and your legacy. A part of Mickey is always with me.

The Gifts of a Teacher

BY BRET STEPHENS

Why teach? More than once in recent years I've heard from teachers, nearing or past retirement, who wondered whether they had chosen the right profession. One thought that maybe she would have done better as an architect. "That way," she said, "at least I could point to something I made."

I suspect that many teachers harbor these sorts of doubts— the wiser the teacher, the graver the doubt. Teaching at its best is less in the business of imparting knowledge than it is of shaping souls. But who can tell what, if anything, has been shaped, much less how well? How much can any single teacher do, in the space of a semester or two, to form the interior spaces of her students' intellectual and emotional lives?

Amy Kass, one of the best teachers I ever had (along with her husband, Leon, also at Chicago), was not immune to these sorts of doubts. She knew that even in the best classrooms at the University of Chicago, with the brightest students in the country, there was a limit to what she could accomplish.

Clever students in her humanities classes could disappoint her, in the way that clever people are often disappointing. A semester's course on Homer's *Odyssey* or Mary Shelley's *Frankenstein* would probably not long stay in the minds of students aiming at careers in law or finance. Even students destined for academic careers of their own were bound to get caught up in everything she disliked about university life: the need to publish, the intellectual faddishness, the petty careerism, the higher cynicism.

Yet for nearly forty years Mrs. Kass persevered, taking the extravagant gamble that every now and then she would find students whose minds would alight with recognition in, say, Levin's feelings for Kitty in *Anna Karenina*, or in Malcolm X's reading of the dictionary in prison, or in Sullivan Ballou's letter to his wife on the eve of the first Battle of Bull Run. These were the students, and such were the texts, that redeemed the enterprise of teaching. They ennobled the profession not because the compensations were many, but because they were few. What's rare is also precious.

What was it like to sit in Mrs. Kass's classroom? The tone was set by the way in which we addressed one another. She was Mrs. Kass (not Dr. Kass, never Amy) to us; we were Mr. Stephens, Ms. Lehman, Mr. Lohse, and so on to her. It was anachronistically formal but radically egalitarian: Whatever our other differences, teacher and student were on an equal footing when it came to discussing the book at hand. We came to class not to be instructed on the meaning of a text (much less Mrs. Kass's views of it), but to read it afresh, without preconceptions. And we read not for the sake of knowledge, but for self-knowledge: to understand ourselves, through stories told by others, as we hadn't fully (or vaguely) understood ourselves before.

Though I never once heard Mrs. Kass utter a political opinion, at the core of her teaching was the belief that, while it's never easy to really know oneself, modern life makes doing so much more difficult. The benefits of emancipation from the old conventions regarding status, sex, manners, and morals may be vast. But they come with hidden costs, notably in the form of aimlessness.

We can satisfy our desires, but we have trouble recognizing our longings. We can do as we please but find it difficult to figure out what truly pleases us, or what we really ought to do. Limitless choice dissipates the possibility of fully realizing the choices we make, whether in our careers or communities or marriages. There's always the chance that something (or someplace, or someone) better is lurking around the corner.

Mrs. Kass believed that at least one aim of a higher education is to provide students with a sextant of sorts, by which they might better discover what it is they should know about life, what they might hope for it, and how they might go about getting it. Not that this belief made her censorious or doctrinaire: You cannot love literature the way she did without also knowing that it is the untidiness of life that makes it interesting. But she cared enough for her students to let them know that the steering aids offered by the modern world might not be enough. Jane Austen still offers the best advice on dating. Aristotle still has the last word on friendship.

About ten years ago Mrs. Kass was diagnosed with ovarian cancer. Last week she succumbed to it, a little shy of her seventy-fifth birthday. Those of us who saw her in the final years never detected a trace of self-pity, an absence of grace, a lack of serious interest in the lives of those she cared for, not least her students. She was a model of what it means to live life wisely, and meaningfully, and—knowing the inevitable limits—fully.

In that sense, Amy Kass's truest teaching was the way in which she chose to lead her life. It left an indelible mark on mine. May her memory be a blessing.

Nature Spirits

Every flower is a soul

blossoming in nature.

—Gerard De Nerval

Old Fir

BY DEBRA D'ANGELO

In August, 2014, my nineteen-year-old daughter, Chiara, climbed a tree on our small island to protest the clear cutting of 830 trees for an unwanted Walgreens. This action inspired many, including Kimberley, a single mom over fifty-nine years old. For weeks Kimberley had been watching tree after tree fall, with men cheering as each one collapsed at their feet. These trees were her community, her protectors, and her inspiration. One particular old fir was closest to her home and viewable through every west-facing window. They had developed a relationship. Old Fir watched through her kitchen window as she prepared meals, watched over her as she slept, and greeted her each morning, filtering the sun just so. Old Fir was one steady and honest force in a life that had proven uncertain.

When the men came to cut Old Fir, Kimberley climbed twelve feet up and sat steady on a branch, eating raw almonds and drinking sweet tea. A scarf tied to a gold velvet bag dangled from the limb where she sat, posting updates to Facebook and texting friends and family to come and offer support. Chiara and I were some of the people she called.

I arrived in the dark, ten hours after she'd climbed the tree, and Kimberley was calm and unwavering. Within an hour of my arrival, plans were made to transition her into a legitimate tree sit, an act of civil disobedience, and she was raised from twelve feet to fifty and secured in a hammock. Kimberley, her eighteen-year-old daughter, and I spent the night with Old Fir and waited.

The police came, the mayor shook her finger and screamed, and the newspapers printed Old Fir's story. A cherry picker came and a man in a uniform was lifted up to Kimberley, but she was not ready to say her final goodbye to Old Fir. She wanted more time. Many birds also came, as did neighbors and supporters. We all told stories of our love for trees and shared our grief in how quickly we were losing them.

I spent two nights and three days under Old Fir, listening to him, watching him, and watching her in his arms.

Old Fir

I saw a towering Old Fir
With rowdy branches, feathers for hair, and coffee-stained teeth.
Arms reaching up to a doorway,
A patch on his left eye,
He seemed to be dancing
and hollering
and asleep
all at the same time.

I understood why she'd chosen him.
Why she had requested one more moment
to rest in his arms
and feel the two winds blow
between their lips.

Her bone-white hair curled around her innocence, like a mermaid or a Queen. It reflected the moon and for two nights none of us slept; it was far too bright.

She'd climbed into his arms, just out of reach,
To let him know
She belonged to him
And he to her.

A proposal of sorts.

Deep into the night she ascended into his dark cave. He wept and welcomed her. All of his stories, a hundred years of wisdom, plus all the creatures he cared for, were now shared between them. On the final morning birds flew in circles above her as if she was Snow White.

He knew she was.

It was a love affair.

He had watched over them, a mother and daughter living without walls. She'd admired him and his was the last face she saw each night before she pulled up the covers. He never slept, and somehow this watchful, one-eyed Fir with the rowdy arms took to her and made a promise.

She wore his ring.

By the third morning, the tyrant circled in and we took up arms. Those of us beneath Old Fir, catching his needles on our wool caps, wanted their love affair to last forever. When we looked up and saw his towering breadth, he seemed a mountain and she a single star.

Time takes its toll and even a Queen must return to the river and her people, especially when one of them is her daughter. The machines and the uniforms were rolling in. The Mayor was screaming.

The Tyrant was taking aim.

The moment collapsed
and within a blink she stood and watched
As he hit the ground.

Her hands still smelled of sap. One of his branches hung, brown and brittle, over the front stoop of the white farm house now surrounded by barren land and stumps.

She couldn't bear the longing. She turned up the music and danced with rowdy arms around the living room and planned for tomorrow.

Looking at Life

BY LEONA PALMER

The smell of pancakes and bacon wafted through the house as you hummed Pink Floyd. The *tink, tink, tink* of tobacco ash emptying into the cut glass tray was followed by the stomp-shuffling from your homemade moccasins crossing the floor. And then the screen door clanging shut.

Past the dewy yard and behind our shed, sat that canvas folding chair patiently looking out at the deep, rolling field that rotated corn, alfalfa, and wheat. At the farthest edge the winding creek bordered a wooded pasture that rose uphill into the southern horizon. Every morning you took a mug of strong, black, "puts hair on your chest" coffee out to your chair to watch the blooming sunrise take the sky and burn the mist off, the blue herons nest and raise their young, the fox skitter across the fields, and the crops grow and then be reaped.

I would sit there next to you, drinking the coffee, which I never drank. We wouldn't talk, but I would watch you watch the earth, your chest rising and falling, like the hills around us. You would turn and smile at me, pointing to something in the distance, and hand me your WWII binoculars. I would hold them up to my eyes and we would look, together, at life.

Coming Home

BY FLORRIE MUNAT

"You're going to have a great around-the-world trip when you scatter my ashes," my husband, Chuck, used to joke, back when those words were a joke. Being thirteen years older than I, Chuck always assumed he would go first.

"Where do you want me to take you?" I would tease back.

"Ireland, Squirrel Island, and Akaroa, of course. Don't forget Akaroa."

I would not forget Akaroa. We had visited that village on each of our six trips to New Zealand. And from Akaroa, our friends Steve and Pam would always take time out from their busy schedules to drive us over the ridgeline behind their sheep farm and down into Flea Bay. The indigenous Maori call this place *Pohatu*, which means "place of stones."

Our love affair with New Zealand began when our family hosted James Travers, an AFS exchange student from Blenheim. Chuck and I made our first journey Down Under in 1982 to witness the wedding celebration of James and his sweetheart, Barbara, and it was Barbara who had first escorted us to her aunt and uncle's sheep farm in Akaroa. It was on that visit that Chuck declared Akaroa to be his favorite place in the world. "When I'm here," he said, "I feel like I'm home."

After that first trip, Chuck broached the idea of moving to New Zealand and though I considered it, I couldn't imagine living 9,000 miles from our family. Chuck was disappointed but understood. He simply vowed we would return often, which we did, five more times. And each time Chuck and I planned our next New Zealand itinerary, we penciled in Akaroa time.

Akaroa and Flea Bay are on the Banks Peninsula—an egg-shaped protrusion into the Pacific Ocean on New Zealand's South Island—and the whole area seemed to be one of those liminal "thin places" where life and not-life mingle in ways no one understands. On each visit, Chuck would survey the cobalt blue waters of the finger-shaped bay, the stony beach, and the decades-old sheep trails dug into the grassy slopes, and say, "I feel like I'm home."

On our first visit to Flea Bay, Steve took Chuck to the rocky shore on the far side of the bay to hunt for little blue penguins. When Steve managed to find two penguins hidden among the rocks, Chuck, an avid birder, was ecstatic. On what turned out to be Chuck's last pilgrimage to New Zealand in 2002, our visit to Flea Bay was glorious but disappointing. When Steve led us on our usual search for little blue penguins, we couldn't find even one. Steve said their absence was one reason he and his brother were working with the Department of Conservation to create a marine reserve at Flea Bay.

A little over a year after we returned home from that visit, Chuck suffered a debilitating stroke, and our lives hurtled into an unfamiliar world of hospitals, rehab, nursing homes, and ultimately a diagnosis of Lewy body dementia, from which he could not recover. He died in 2009.

I knew I would one day spread his ashes in Akaroa, but it took three years before I was ready. During my solo trip to New Zealand, I was repeatedly shocked every time I realized I was there without Chuck.

I began that visit at James's home in Wellington. Then we drove to Akaroa, where Pam and Steve greeted us with hugs of welcome and words of condolence for Chuck. Sitting in their sunny yard that afternoon, I heard bellbirds warbling and native pigeons rustling in the evergreens, and my heart ached because he wasn't there to say, "I feel like I'm home."

The next morning dawned gray and drizzly. I heard a knock at my door and opened it to find Pam, who caroled, "Happy Birthday!" I hadn't planned on being in Akaroa for my sixty-fifth, but that seemed like an appropriate blessing. After a breakfast of tea and toast, Steve, Pam, James, and I made the drive to Flea Bay, thirty years after Chuck and I had first seen it. I sat in the back seat holding a Native American cedar box containing Chuck's ashes.

We passed the Garden of Tane, and I remembered our walks through the native bush with Steve and Pam's children and our youngest son, Teddy, who is a father now himself. I saw every tree, road sign, and bend in the road through Chuck's eyes, because he had loved this place, and the thought of being without him for the rest of my life was almost unbearable. Though my chest hurt from holding back my sobs, I didn't want to dampen the day for the others, so I stared at my hands and tried not to think about where we were headed.

As Steve made the last sweeping turn and headed down toward the bay, Pam turned to me. "That box has made a long journey to get here, hasn't it, Florrie? Quite a pilgrimage." Her words loosened something within me, and I began to weep. I wanted Chuck to be next to me, just as he had always been, not ashes in a box.

The plan was for us to use an inflatable boat to go out into the bay. But a sheep had run away with the boat's bung (plug), so we decided to use Steve and Pam's kayaks instead. I'd never been in a kayak, but it seemed appropriate to try something new on this day. We slipped on flotation vests and carried two yellow kayaks from a boat-shed to the beach. Steve got Pam situated in one kayak, and James and I got into the other. The water was calm and cold. We pulled away from the shore, and with strong strokes Steve and James propelled the kayaks to the middle of the bay. Again I let my tears flow, and this time they felt cleansing on my cheeks.

We brought the kayaks side by side. I removed the lid from the cedar box, opened the bag, and released Chuck's ashes into the water, which was somehow dappled with light despite the clouds. As the ashes sank into the gray-green depths, I realized my tears had stopped.

Back at Steve and Pam's house, I gave them the cedar box. In return, Steve gave me an abstract oil painting he'd done of Akaroa Harbour. The clouds, hills, and water are painted in shades of gold, mustard, pale blue, royal blue, brown, and ivory. The valley next to their farm was painted in the darkest shade of blue imaginable, almost black. Steve said that Maoris call this place *Oteauheke*, which means "place where the mist comes down." It is their sacred burial ground. "There's been a lot of sadness here," he explained. "The sorrows of the Maoris who were forced off the land. The hardships the settlers suffered while they toiled on these hills." Near the bottom of the canvas, Steve had allowed the paint to drip. "The drips represent the tears that have been shed here."

And mine are a part of that now, I thought.

Leaving New Zealand is always a sorrow, as Chuck knew only too well. It is so far away, you never know when you'll be back.

And if you do return, you don't know who will be left to greet you. In 2002, Chuck and James's mother, Gladys, promised they'd try to stick around for another visit, but neither was able to keep that promise. So at the Wellington Airport when James and I shared a final hug, we both shed a few tears before he turned and walked quickly away.

The morning was still dark when I boarded my flight to Sydney. But the moment the plane lifted off the tarmac, orange light from the rising sun burst through the cabin windows, momentarily blinding me. And I thought, *You're home now, Chuck.*

A few weeks after I returned to America, Pam wrote to say that three hundred pairs of nesting little blue penguins had just been counted among the rocks at Flea Bay in the new Pohatu Marine Reserve. *Welcome home.*

Spider

BY JUDITH PACHT

she hangs

between
    drywall & cement
    floor & painted wall
    inside her tangled mess

resting
    belly up & naked
    private parts
        exposed

her crimson birthmark
calls out
her name

I wonder if she's weary
    her day filled
    spinning
        fetching a silk taste
           a fly-by
caught in a cycle   spinning

me
    I scoop lint
    from the dryer   weather
    strip a leaky window

quotidian comforts
    kill what's precious

both of us
> intimate assassins
>
> spinning

to cover
> death's dark cheek
> > his scratch & stubble
> >
> > > the ink-black
> > > deep in the iris of his eye

Song of the Tree Frog

BY G. ELIZABETH KRETCHMER

The Pacific Tree Frogs came out each spring in Central Oregon, while the winter clouds still thickened the sky, the wind still blew from somewhere up north, and snow still draped the peaks of the higher Cascades. We all complained about how cold it was, how long the winter had been. We'd grown tired of isolating ourselves, of burrowing deep into our homes. But once we heard the frogs' chorus in our backyards—a pandemonium of joyful chirps and lusty croaks—it seemed that hope had returned.

The congregation of frogs is a family reunion. They meet up at the same pond where their forebears have gathered, a place where they feel they belong, a place that's instinctively secure. The males sing their songs of desire; the females come to the amphibious bedroom. The group assembly raises the local temperature and humidity, for the greater good of all, until new eggs are laid and the adults are free to—or required to—move on.

Just as springtime mating is predictable for frogs, moving seemed to become a predictable pattern in our lives, so much so that I occasionally wondered if my husband was descended from a band of nomads. Our first move was away from the century-old farmhouse outside of Portland, Oregon, that I'd bought before we were married, back when I was in my twenties. It sat, along with a weather-worn red barn, on the remaining five acres of what was once a 400-acre homestead, overlooking lush sheep-grazing pastures and offering a panoramic explosion of western sky. I had my own sheep, a thriving herb garden, and a scraggly old orchard. Cattle mooed on neighboring properties; peacocks periodically escaped from a nearby farm to mine; skunk kits tumbled with one another in my yard; daffodils volunteered throughout the pastures. My three cats faithfully brought dead mice to me, like children bringing home freshly picked dandelions. It was practically heaven.

But not necessarily for the family we planned to build.

"We should move," my husband said over dinner one night,

as logs cut from ancient fruit trees crackled in the fireplace behind him. "We should move to a regular house in a regular neighborhood, near schools and playgrounds, to a community where we can raise our kids and they can have friends." I resented the idea that he could sit there in what had been *my* farm and suggest a move, but he made some good points, especially since the farm was miles away from everything. There were no children nearby, no swimming pools, no soccer fields—and no heat in the bedrooms on cold winter nights. He wanted to live in a place where we could be comfortable and live a normal suburban lifestyle, where our kids could have the best of everything. Although I loved the quietude of my farm, which was the complete opposite of the hubbub of my hometown Chicago, I eventually gave in, exchanging my need for solitude for the needs of our unborn children. It was a plan that seemed right.

Our next house was in the southwest suburbs of Portland. It was brand new and, perched atop a steep hill, it offered sweeping views of rain clouds. We adopted our first son less than a year after we moved there, and by the time he was two years old, he'd learned to appreciate the view at night, which—when the skies were clear—he called "lights in the distance." We took our son to Gymboree classes and playgroups; we ran the baby jogger up and down the winding streets; we invited our parents to visit this new place we intended to call home for a long time. But in our naiveté we hadn't realized that such a hilly, steep neighborhood wouldn't be conducive to learning to ride a tricycle, and we soon discovered there were few children living close at hand.

"We should move," my husband said again. As much as I hated to uproot our little family, I had to agree this neighborhood wasn't ideal. And because we were well-educated parents who had begun to drink society's Kool-Aid notion that we must offer our children the very best we possibly could, no matter the cost, we bought a vacant lot farther out from Portland in an even newer subdivision. It afforded panoramic views of the Cascades, which was important to me, and the neighborhood was built on a flat plateau—perfect for little guys riding tricycles. New schools, parks, and retail stores within walking distance were already under construction, assuring us this would indeed be the perfect place to finally settle.

We crammed into a small rental house while our new house was being built. I took our son out to the construction site daily, where he played with toy trucks in the loose dirt and rode the bulldozer with the contractor. I took him shopping for light fixtures, flooring, tile, and doorknobs. He picked out a rich blue hue for the walls of his room, asked if we could build a play structure in the back yard, and wondered aloud where other little boys might soon live.

But just as that house was coming to completion, my husband was offered a job in California.

"We should move," he said.

"You're not seriously considering this offer," I said. "Are you?" We were getting ready for bed. He held up his toothbrush and tried to answer with a mouth full of foamy toothpaste. It sounded like "WlallyImm."

"What?"

He finished brushing for a torturously long time, then spit and rinsed and tapped his toothbrush against the side of the sink. "Well, actually I am."

We agreed to sleep on the matter, although sleep did not come easily to me. I rode the roller coaster of worry for the next several days, my stomach upset at the thought of leaving everything and everyone behind, of leaving Oregon. I loved the brilliant rhododendrons in the city, the peekaboo games Mt. Hood played, the rivers and woodsy trails. I even loved the ice storms and the fog. Oregon was my home. And our son's home too. The thought of moving terrified me.

Our son had already been transplanted a couple of times, and because he was an adopted child, I knew he needed extra security, extra stability. To leave the place that he knew as home— not just a particular yard or neighborhood but an entire climate and culture—seemed like a lot for a boy not yet three years old. I checked in with his pediatrician.

"As long as he's with you, that's what counts," the doctor said. "Kids adapt."

We spent the next five years in the San Francisco area, living in the shadow of Mt. Diablo. We adopted two more sons while there, and our oldest son did indeed adapt. He made new friends, went to school, learned to swim and ski, and developed a passion for rock climbing. Clearly, California had proven itself to be fine for him and our other boys. But it had its drawbacks, including a rising cost of living, tightened restrictions on corporations, and increasingly congested highways.

"We should move."

"There's no f@#!ing way I'm going to move again," I said, when the kids weren't listening, of course. But my husband's usual persuasive tactics began to infiltrate my thoughts, and I was, truth be told, pretty sick and tired of the traffic. Finally, I told him there was one, and only one, condition in which I'd consider moving.

At 4:30 the next morning, I woke up to my husband gently shaking my shoulders. It was still dark outside; I couldn't imagine what the emergency might be.

"I've been up all night on the Internet," he said. "You've got to come see this."

I shuffled upstairs to our den, sat down bleary-eyed in front of the computer, and saw all sorts of websites and information about Bend, Oregon. He had listened to me when I'd said the only way I'd uproot our family again would be if we returned to Oregon.

"But I meant Portland," I said as I wandered, zombielike, into the kitchen for coffee. "Not Central Oregon."

Within a week, after studying academic and enrichment opportunities there—still determined to offer the best we possibly could to our children—and after recalling numerous weekends we'd spent in Sunriver (just south of Bend), I found my heart pumping the way it does when you're about to reconnect with a long lost lover. I needed our oldest son to be on board, though. He was the one who had been moved around the most. He was also the one who most readily attached to people, things, and places. And the other two boys were, at that stage, too young to really comprehend what moving was all about.

"I want to show you around Central Oregon," I said as I packed him into the car. "If you like it, we might move there."

I braced myself for whining, but he didn't question, complain, or flinch. He kept his nose pressed to the window for much of the ten-hour road trip. We crossed into the sprawling land of cheat grass and sage and juniper, a palette of desert hues I've found nowhere else on earth. I watched him in my rearview mirror as he watched a tumbleweed bounce along the road's shoulder with a sort of meditative anticipation resting on his face.

As for me, I knew one thing to be true: I was coming home to the place I belonged, the way salmon return to Oregon's freshwater rivers after living out in the ocean for years.

Less than a month after that trip, we had moved back to Oregon once again, with our son's enthusiastic blessing. We settled on twenty acres outside of Bend with plenty of open space where the boys could freely roam and explore, hunt for scorpions and obsidian, hide out in lava caves, climb rock cliffs and towering fir trees, and do whatever else boys do when faced with plenty of time, land, and dirt. We joined a growing, vibrant community that shared many of the same values we did, particularly a love of the outdoors. And we had a pond that was home to dozens of frogs each spring.

But, as they say, change is inevitable.

"We should move," my husband proposed one cold, winter day after nearly ten years in Central Oregon. As with other times he'd proposed such changes, he had good reasons—reasons that yet again had to do with what he felt was best for the kids. We fought, and I cried, and then I acquiesced. But this time our oldest son, now eighteen, didn't.

"I'm not moving," he said, his arms outstretched Charlie Brown style. "This is my home and you can't make me move." As much as I didn't want to leave him behind, I was proud of his courageous stance. And touched that he wanted to stay put. Oregon was where he felt he belonged, and I understood now, more than ever, the importance of feeling connected to one's place.

My two younger sons agreed to the move, so with a vote of three to two, I went along with the decision. Sometimes you have to let go of what you love, for the greater good.

As we prepared for the house to sell in the spring, I returned to Bend for a few weeks to pack up the belongings we'd left behind and to help my son move out of the house. As I set aside plates and other furnishings for his new apartment, I found myself worrying about whether he was really ready to grow up and be on his own. Whether he'd eat right and take care of himself, whether he'd find a job or have enough friends. Whether he'd know what to do if the toilet clogged. Whether he'd miss me.

And, most of all, whether his new apartment would possibly feel like home for him.

One evening, as I was packing royalty members and pawns from our living room chess set, I heard the first few frogs croaking at various pitches, like vocalists warming up before a concert. Then, in a matter of seconds, the collection of rambunctious voices rose rhythmically. I set down the queen, left my packing cartons and paper behind, and hurried to the deck overlooking our pond, where the amphibious music—and all the memories from raising our children there in the high desert—rushed through me viscerally, like warm blood.

As the days passed, the quantity of packed boxes increased, but the frogs' songs lessened. On my last night, I went downstairs to check on my son's packing progress. Heavy metal music pounded from behind his closed and locked door. I leaned against his door, gently, and imagined him sitting behind it on the floor, surrounded by a clutter of favorite books, vacation souvenirs, and moving boxes. And then I heard his deep, grown voice singing along with the angry music he loved.

Back upstairs, a solitary amphibian song rang out in the high desert night. I stepped outside and listened, imagining that this frog wasn't ready to move away, either. He didn't want to know the grief of leaving, of becoming separated from the place he'd known as home. Instead, he would hold the grief for all the others that had already gone, according to the master plan, and he would stay up all night in that place where he most belonged, singing.

As Nature Intended

BY BENJAMIN GREENSPOON

I live in Seattle, one of the most densely populated cities in the country. I use nature as a way to escape the horrors and unfortunate events going on where I am living. Backpacking and engaging in conservation work offers me the alone and quiet time I need as well as giving me the opportunity to enjoy nature at its fullest.

Last summer I went on a backpacking trip with the Student Conservation Association—the organization that I volunteer with—to the Olympic Coast. The goal of the mission was to remove as much debris from the beach as we could. The group consisted of eight students and two leaders from various parts of United States. Whether from rural farmland in the Midwest or cities like Detroit and New York, most of the students had never hiked farther than two miles. Some of us were there for our appreciation of nature, but others were merely trying to fulfill their high school community service requirement. The car ride from Seattle to the Olympic National Park was silent, as ten strangers privately wondered what the next two weeks would entail.

The trip began at the trail head, about eight miles from the coast. We strapped on our humongous backpacks, instantly hunched over with forty pounds attached to our backs, and began to hike. For hours we looked at the horizon, hoping the forest would open up. For hours we hoped to see waves brushing up against the beach, signifying we were at our campsite. For hours we wished we could take off our packs. Finally, the trail ended, and the horizon of the sky met with the ocean. We finally made it.

It looked like a picture on a postcard—vast, pristine, wild. But once I walked on to the beach, the picture-perfect image faded and was replaced by McDonald's kids' meal toys, soda cans, and Windex window cleaner bottles. Hundreds of plastic bottles and fishing ropes were scattered up and down the beach, lying next to hundreds of products manufactured in China.

After days of picking up garbage off the beach, it was time to haul it out. Along with hundreds of filled-to-capacity trash bags, we also had many abandoned appliances to remove. We strapped the trash bags together and threw them on buoys that we found washed up on the shore, tying everything together with rope that we attached around our waists. With our "sleds" dragging behind us, we started the eight-mile hike back to the car. The additional fifty pounds of trash, along with the forty pounds already on our backs, and eighty-degree weather drove our crew nearly to a breaking point. A sharp pain jolted all the way from my lower back to my neck, eventually causing me to have to go to the hospital. But the trip was still worth it, and I'd do it again for the reward of being able to offer people the postcard version of the beach. A place where they can experience all that nature offers and none of the detritus from mankind.

Along the Way

BY DAVE REECK

In the summer of 2016, I rode 1,546 miles of the Tour
Divide—the world's longest mountain bike race—and
left many things behind.

Backup, backup GPS—the Banff YWCA
Mailed home at 3:00 a.m. on the morning of the start
Broken battery contact made it a fancy paperweight

A jar of Nutella, a bag of granola—Bolton trading post in
Alberta
Left on a table in the rain
Bear food

Two pairs of gloves and some knee warmers—the cabin at
Elk Pass
Left on top of a cooling wood stove
Pushed out of mind by fourth tire repair in two days

A sewing needle—unnamed forest road in British Columbia
Vanished in the scrub brush
Twenty minutes of panicked searching turned up nothing

My malfunctioning rear tire—Elkford, B.C.
Into the dumpster it went
Good riddance. I'd have used a wood chipper if I'd seen one

Bike saddle rivet—Flathead Valley Road, B.C.
Sprung free while riding along
A zip tie repair

A plastic fender—dirt road, Montana
Hurled over the fence at a transfer station
I salute you, plastic fender—you had one job to do and you
did it well

Fourteen ounces of Ensure meal replacement drink—three
   miles south of Holland Lake
Poured on to the ground
It became clear I'd made yogurt rather than a wise nutrition
   decision

My wallet—Duhnam Creek Road
Slipped from my pocket while talking with friendly locals
Returned by passersby, courtesy of my stupendous good
   luck

Twenty pounds of me—Yampa Valley
Registered on the regional airport luggage scale
Don't you worry, I'll find it again

Walking Distance

BY MARIANNE GOLDSMITH

Dear David,
 Today we drove into the Oakland hills to hike in Huckleberry Botanic Preserve. A favorite of yours.

I followed my husband down a trail of pale, dry leaves, trees overhead saturated with green. Maybe we'd been here before, taking this pathway bleached in sunlit patches, brilliant lime ferns clustered in long fringes.

Climbing a steeper grade, the distant landscape of soft, grassy hills appeared behind branches and thick, arching trunks. Round another bend, stepping over dark roots and leaves, we entered a broad bowl surrounded by earthen walls, lined with multi-pronged trunks of bay trees, fallen logs decomposing among scattered pockets of ferns.

You probably had deadlines, came here to take a break, get out of your head. Did you know the trail so well, learned it by heart, as you would a poem or favorite song? Had it become as familiar as the way home, where you lived with your wife, where together you raised your children, holding on to them, letting go, as their growth demanded? Did you come here to absorb the solitude, listening to overlapping sounds of bird songs, the wind lifting branches, rolling, shaking the outermost tips of leaves?

And then someone cut you off, tore your life out from under you, clipped in less time than it takes to read this sentence.

Five months passed before I read online coverage of the homicide. On that November afternoon in the park, hikers heard gunshots. A woman found you lying on the ground. Sketches of two "persons of interest" were included in news bulletins. What scalded me was your portrait, brown eyes gazing calmly at the camera. You looked trim, vigorous, with white hair, mustache, and beard.

We had lost touch since you and your family first moved here from the Midwest in the late 1990s. I remember bringing maps of California to your home in the Oakland hills, describing the beauty of the wilderness within reach. Instructing you in seismic decorating principles: never hang anything above your bed.

We were both intense talkers. Our conversations ran overtime, each staking out a claim and ready to wrangle. Our partners and children had long abandoned the table as we dug into issues, politics, prophecies.

Our connection might have endured, had I been more restrained, less opinionated. A conflict developed between us. I hesitated too long to repair our friendship. Though you once described me as "intrepid," I was stretched too thin, mired in a family problem that turned into a crisis.

I knew you as a fine, sincere writer, a loving husband and father. How moving to read your students' tributes online and watch videos of fellow parishioners who cherished you, to see your new grandbaby, bobbing up and down on his wobbly legs, his fingers clinging to his mother's hands.

And now my journey on the Huckleberry Trail, loping into a footfall rhythm, ducking in and out of deepening shade and stark sunlight, skirting steep ravines choked with rocks, ferns, and branches, surrounded by high-pitched calls from the slender throats of birds. Tight leg muscles began to relax, my arms hanging more freely. Who wouldn't abandon a desk for this walk? It's the constant demand that wears us down, pushing to say it right, stringing together piles, layers of words, discarding them like dry leaves, forming, re-forming new phrases to map out ideas, carry our dreams.

On the trail back, my husband and I crossed paths with several couples and a few families, the kids eager to run ahead of their parents. We were approaching the end of the trail, hiking uphill along a ridge, when I noticed my left hand clasped, as if holding on—to what? I let go, but it felt wrong. I needed to grasp, hold on, as if, through this transitory, "paranormal" sensation, you were close, and I was holding that thread for you.

In memory of David Ruenzel

Moments Collapse

BY WILL SILVERMAN

Moments collapse
Into an atmosphere
Densely packed and shifting
Through a horizontal plane

Pass gently through sky
Touch the aurora borealis
Absorb sparks of daylight
As they kiss the coming rain

Kiss the coming rain

Your lessons duly learned
Now you etch your name
In starlight as you dance
Among seeds of time

Embrace the passage
For you have left
Your mark in thunderclaps
And whispers of wind

Whisper to the wind

Let me shoulder
Your load as you roll
Through toils and trials
Until dreams call you home

And if I haven't said
These words aloud

"Thank you"
Let me share them today

Share them today

Slip silent
As mysteries unfold
Let loose of that opening door
Step deliberately along

Legacies live on
Through children and clouds
Spring shares brilliant sun
Bitterroots bloom again

Bloom again

On a Mountain

BY WILL SILVERMAN

Doggedly chasing the past

I have to ask forgiveness

Mom, years went by without you

I doubt a day went by that you didn't

Dream of sharing hours with three

Minds and souls you brought

Home on stormy nights

Some horizons couldn't shelter you

From shattered glass

Broken promises, foggy Irish mornings

We sifted through mist

And watched in silence

As you slowly drifted on

Four broken hearts left unglued

Used up and worn

Torn from illusion, you moved

Caught in a jet stream, seamless and certain

That no other choice would suffice

Rebuilding from sand, in your own terms

Apart from those that you loved

You journeyed on

And in this moment, time catches us

Alive, awake and miles away

Nothing says hello like "hello"

In the hollow of an echo

I hear you, in the whistling wind

Through a Montana canyon, you sing

That *Carousel* song in the rain

I remember

I Would Like to Say

Kind words can be short and easy to speak, but their echoes are truly endless.

—Mother Teresa

Afraid of the Question

BY J. R. MILLER

There's so much I can't remember about us. About you. From back then, all those years ago. You were the pastor's boy. That's what the adults called you, "the pastor's boy," not Todd. I always found this strange. Why not the pastor's son? After all, five kids, and you were his only son. You were the one expected to carry out the family name.

We were both thirteen; you were three months older and half a foot taller. It was early summer and we were swimming in your freezing cold pool. *Marco. Polo.* Your sister, the one with blonde hair, and her friends lay around on the lounge chairs trying to catch a tan. Soon she would be old enough to drive her friends to the beach, where the older boys lay in wait. But now, they giggled and talked about girl stuff in hushed whispers. One of your sister's friends stood up and walked to the edge of the pool, bent over to feel the water—her boobs practically falling out of her bikini top. I stared at them. You stared at them. When she stood back up, complaining that the water was way too cold, she caught us.

"You like what you see, boys?" she asked. She licked her lips, like all those MTV video girls, and lowered the string to one side of her top. She let her breast slide out so that we could see the whole of it, uninhibited.

We stared.

Your sister got angry. "The little squealer's gonna tell my dad," she complained. "And I'm gonna get grounded." I wondered which one of us she considered the little squealer. Her friend covered up and walked back to her chair. Before she sat, she asked, "You aren't gonna tell the preacher man on me—are you, boys?" I shook my head no. We both did.

I had a crush on your sister; well, all of your sisters, but the one with blonde hair was my favorite. She was the closest to our age, only two years older. Still, I never told her. I doubt she would have cared that her baby brother's little friend liked her—not then, when we were thirteen, not when we were fourteen—and not a few years later, when I saw her and her boyfriend at the mall—a few months after your funeral.

I regret not talking to her that day as she let her boyfriend buy her a pretzel. I could've said, should've said, "I'm really sorry for your loss." I could've given her a hug and said, "Todd was a great guy." Should've.

I was afraid—afraid of the question. Not the one where she asked, "Why didn't you come to the funeral?" Not the one where she asked, "Why did you stop hanging out with Todd? You two were such good friends." No, those questions were easy—sort of. I was afraid of, "Do you know why he did it?"

I don't know why you did it. Not really. You didn't seem the type, not when we were friends. When we were friends, you pretended to be a normal teenage boy. But then didn't we all pretend to be normal—just a little?

Sometimes, when I'm thinking about things, things like this, like you, I wish I could remember better. I want to remember some of the small details, like your last name, your sister's name, the one with blonde hair, even her friend's name, the one who showed us her boob. But more importantly, I wish I could remember what we used to talk about back then—when we were friends. I wish I could remember why I thought we were such good friends—why everybody thought we were such good friends.

My mom took me to your dad's church—that's how we met. The church was an old elementary school converted to sanctuary. In the gym, under the basketball hoop, your dad saved my mom, showed her the path to everlasting life. He told me I needed to accept Jesus Christ as my personal Lord, and I did, because back then I listened, I did what I was told.

After I was saved, I was sent to the youth group; that's where you were and a few of your sisters and that girl Carla, the one who got pregnant, and that older boy, Sean. He was fifteen or sixteen, right? You thought he was cool because he could grow a mustache and wore muscle shirts and because he actually had muscles. His arms weren't skin-covered sticks like ours.

Every Sunday, after youth group, while our moms gossiped and your dad tended to the flock, we played board games, goofed around, and talked. Once, during a game of checkers, you told me about your secret girlfriend.

Your dad was serious about sin. He wanted no one in his congregation to backslide. He used to tell us all the time, "Check your heart." He used to say, "Root out that evil. If you die in sin, then you shall inherit hell for all of eternity."

There was that one Sunday when youth group was cancelled and we all had to sit in with the adults. Since that girl Carla got pregnant, your dad felt it was imperative for us to hear his sermon on lust and sex. For nearly two hours, he quoted Old Testament—about spilling of seed and lying with men. He preached about lust of the flesh and he systematically told us how bad sex was. That it was sin. "Masturbation, sin. Looking at porn, sin. Lusting," he said, "over the guys or girls at school, or at work, or even here in the holy sanctuary, it's all sin." He rattled it all off, louder and louder—sex before marriage, oral sex, kissing: sin. "Homosexuality," he roared, "sin." And he slammed his Bible closed. "And sin," he finished in a quieter, more dad-like voice, "is the pathway to your soul's destruction."

After the sermon, while you jumped my last king and left me with one last trapped checker, I asked if you knew what oral sex was, and you whispered that you thought it was when you talked about sex.

"What? Really? You can't even talk about it?"

You laughed. "No," you said. "Oral sex is a blow job."

I laughed along with you and said, "Ohhh," like I knew what a blow job was.

Did I ever tell you? Shortly after I joined your dad's church, I lost all my friends from the neighborhood—all the kids I'd played with since my family moved on the block in second grade. And that loss was sudden. One night, inches and inches of fresh new snow fell from the sky, and the next morning—no school. The guys all came down and we played tackle football on the front lawn. We spent most of the morning shoving our friends' faces deep in the snow. Scooping fistfuls of the white powder and dumping it inside the collars of thick winter coats. And then my mom made lunch for us all. But before we could eat our peanut butter on week-old store-brand white bread, we had to say prayers.

"Like grace?" my friend David asked.

"No, not grace," my mom said. "That's what those Catholics do. No, there will be none of that. We need real prayer. You all need to pray to Jesus. All of you need to accept Jesus into your heart." And for a long time my mother told my friends, the kids I used to go to catechism with, about the absolute necessity of turning their lives over to the Lord and the sin of being Catholic.

After prayer, we sat quietly eating our sandwiches—the bread a little hard from sitting too long in the dry heat of furnaced air.

When we were allowed to go back outside, my friends decided they wanted to go down the road to the playground. I said, "Hold on," and ran in to ask for permission.

By the time I negotiated permission and raced back outside, they were gone. I ran to catch up. I ran all the way to the park—my cheeks numb, my ears throbbing, and my lungs closing from the cold—but nobody was there. The snow was still fresh and untouched.

I wondered about other things. I wondered how you could keep your girlfriend a secret from your dad. I wondered why I didn't know your girlfriend's name. I wondered about that girl Carla, the one who got pregnant. Was it possible she was your girlfriend? It's not that big of a stretch. I mean, after all, you knew that oral sex was a blow job and you knew what a blow job was. But then, if you were having sex, wouldn't you tell me—because that's what best friends do, right? They tell each other things they can't tell anyone else.

At the beginning of my first all-night lock-in with the youth group, the boys had to fold and stack all the chairs set up for church service, so at midnight both boys and girls could spread out our sleeping bags on the floor and sleep—girls on the visitor side of the court, boys on the home side, next to the altar. There was basketball and dodge ball for hours. Pizza, chips, and pop. The youth leader, Karl, brought his boom box and we listened to Christian music loud and proud. We even got to watch a video on TV. The tape was a church movie, but still, it was TV—a rare treat for many of us. Of course there was Bible reading and praying, but, by now, that was so much a part of life every day, like brushing teeth.

While you picked off your pepperoni and tossed them on my plate, you told me more about your girlfriend. You said you kissed her a bunch of times. You said that kissing another person, real kissing, was awesome. You said that it's best when you both chew different kinds of gum or eat different candy, and then you try and guess the flavor when you French kiss. I can admit it now: I thought you were lying. Seriously, guess the flavor of somebody's tongue? I asked who this mystery girl was. "And when," I asked, "could you possibly have the opportunity to kiss her?" You just laughed, said, "That's my secret."

When we were ready to play basketball, you and that older kid, Sean, were picked captains. You picked me first, because we were best friends and only a best friend would pick me, the second shortest and by far the worst basketball player in the building. We lost three straight games because I kept passing to kids who weren't on our team. And because the guys were getting pissed at me, you said, "No worries." You told the team it wasn't my fault, it was Karl's because he wouldn't let us play shirts and skins, and it's too hard to know who's on your team when everyone's wearing the same "Christ is King" navy-blue T-shirt.

During the third game, you took an elbow from Sean, to the side of the face, and it knocked you flat. After he offered his hand and helped you to your feet, he gave you the ball and said, "Take your shots; that was completely a foul." Except, it wasn't.

In prayer circle that night, when we each had to offer up something to pray for, Sean offered up your face in prayer; he asked for a fast healing. And then you offered up his elbow, that the next time it would stop before striking someone. And everyone laughed. I was angry with you, or jealous, over this banter. Then it was my turn and I had nothing.

I don't know how you did it. It's not that I forgot; I simply never asked. On purpose. I didn't want to know. I don't want to know. Though I do hope you chose sleeping pills or carbon monoxide. I hope you chose something that let you peacefully go to sleep.

I do wonder if you left a letter. A note. I wonder if you placed blame on others, indicted those who failed you. I wonder if I'm in that letter. I should be. All those years ago, that one night, I could have chosen to be a friend, accepted you for you, but, instead, I taunted you, then walked away—hid from sight until I could make you disappear.

Even with the pregnant Carla controversy, even though I was *still* grounded for a bad grade on my last report card, my mom let me go to the "end-of-summer" lock-in. She said I could use a break. I did deserve a break. For most of that summer, instead of riding my bike, or skateboarding, or swimming, I had to sit at the kitchen table writing scripture. That summer I wrote all of Psalms, all of Proverbs, and I wrote all of Revelation, twice. I also wrote in repetition the Ten Commandments. Each commandment I wrote 1,000 times. I wrote 10,000 commandments and I wrote John 3:16 500 times. By that night, the end-of-summer lock-in, my left hand and forearm were taut writing machines, while the rest of me was pasty and weak and angry.

That night was the last night we were friends. We stacked the chairs, we turned over our five bucks for the pizza and pop, and we picked teams for basketball. Karl was captain this time, and you. And there was a lot of smack-down between you two. A bet was placed. The losing team had to set the chairs back up in the morning. You picked first. You picked Sean; I took a step forward before understanding that my name wasn't Sean. I stepped back. Karl picked David. You picked Chris. Chris? Karl picked Bobby. You Travis, he Dennis, you Tony, he Shane, you Corey. And there I stood: the last man standing.

I wish I could say that my anger drove me to play better. It didn't. I wish I could say that I contributed to your team's loss. I didn't. But I cherished the win nonetheless. After the game, Karl led our team in prayer, giving thanks for our victory.

Later, after prayer, after scripture, we ate pizza and you acted like everything was cool. You challenged me to checkers. Sean said, "Later, we could play poker." He told us he brought three rolls of Neccos. "We can use them for chips." Then one of the girls knocked over a pop bottle—spilled Faygo Redpop all over the floor. Karl sent you to get the mop. In the chaos of a girly squeal and laughing and five or six people scrambling with piles of cheap napkins to absorb the sticky redness before it spread, nobody noticed Sean went with you.

After five minutes, you still had not returned with the mop, and Karl called for me to go find you, "Now. And tell him I said to hustle."

I ran out of the gym and toward the maintenance closet. The closet was in the toddler wing and there were no lights on. The halls were dark with darker shadows. I slowly walked down one long hall, then turned left toward the closet.

In the shadows, I can't be sure what I saw. Not really. But there you guys were, kissing. You and Sean. Kissing. He had you pressed up against the wall. His face close to yours. Kissing.

I didn't say anything. I didn't make a sound. I turned back and walked to the gym. I crept back to the table. I told myself that this wasn't really happening. It was dark. I didn't see what I saw. Couldn't have. You were both boys. Boys don't kiss boys. Boys kiss girls. You kiss girls. You told me so. You told me a lot of things.

A couple of minutes later you walked in, wheeling the mop bucket—hot water steaming. You mopped the floor. Sean put up the wet floor signs, and when everything was cleaned up to Karl's standards, you both put everything back in the closet.

Later that night, after the church video, you asked if I wanted to play a game of checkers. I said, "No." You gave me a look, one that said, "What did I do?" You never asked me, but still the look said everything. I said, "I don't want to play checkers with you." I said, "Maybe you should go ask *him* to play with you."

"Ask who?"

"Who do you think?"

I wonder if you ever got into a fight. A real fight—against another boy—hands balled up into tight fists and thrown toward the face or the stomach. Did you ever punch somebody? I don't think you did. But you should have. You should have punched me that night. I said, "Who do you think?" and I puckered my lips in an exaggerated kissy-face and kissed the air three times with as much anger and hatred as I could muster. You should've punched me. Right there, on the basketball court, standing before the altar, with the chaos of teen frolic, in front of everyone, in front of no one. I would have punched you back. We would have fought. Sean would have pulled you off me. Karl would have pulled me off you. My eye would blacken while your nose bled and neither of us would answer Karl—neither of us would tell him why exactly we were fighting. Karl would make us shake. He'd make us ask for forgiveness, he'd make us forgive. And things might have gone back to normal. Instead you stood there, wobbling on your feet like somebody just punched *you*, face bloodless, eyes wet like you were going to cry. You stood there and I walked away.

"His funeral is tomorrow," they said. They asked if I wanted to come and pray for your soul. I don't remember how old I was: eighteen or nineteen, I think. So you were eighteen or nineteen. I quit going to your dad's church long before then, and by then I had written off God and Jesus.

They told me you were still part of the church and that you had been fighting your demons but lost. They told me like I cared about demons. They said you'd been fighting them for years. They charged you with being an alcoholic and a drug abuser. They said there were whispers, there were rumors and allegations in the congregation that you were a homosexual. They said that the ladies in the prayer group found out that your dad caught you naked with another guy. They said the pastor went down in the basement of your childhood home for some paper towels, or dish soap, or hamburger from the deep freeze, and there you were, with a guy, engaged in oral sex—a blow job.

They thought that was why you killed yourself. Maybe they were right. Maybe you couldn't shake the image of your father at the moment, the look he had on his face. Maybe that's what you could not live with. Or maybe it was just the last straw.

Back when I saw your sister with her boyfriend, buying a pretzel, I wondered if she knew why we stopped being friends. I didn't say anything to her. When I said I was afraid of her question, I was lying. I was afraid of my answer. Truth is, I hadn't been your friend in many years. I didn't know you anymore. I don't think I ever did, not really. But still, I wonder, if we could've shook hands that night, with bloody noses and black eyes, then maybe things would have turned out a little better for you. Maybe that would have been enough.

I wondered what Bible story your dad would use to help soothe the flock. I thought it would be fitting if he chose the parable of the prodigal son, where the father forgives the lost boy for his transgressions. Or maybe the story of the adulterer—the one where Jesus says, "He that is without sin..." Or maybe the one where Peter betrays Jesus, not once, not twice, but three times—before the cock crowed.

That day, they told me they were glad that God had given *me* the wisdom to move away from you—given *me* the wisdom to choose friends with better character. Wisdom and character. "Do you want to go? You can ride with us."

"What's the point?" I said.

"You can pray for him," they said that day, all those years ago. "It takes more than being the pastor's boy to get into heaven."

"Son," I said. "Todd was the pastor's son."

Sorry

BY BARBARA EKNOIAN

Sometimes you can't
make something
right again
with all the resolve
you may have.

You might place
the flower
on her grave
and whisper what's
in your heart,
but she's in the ground
and can't hear you.

Your regret remains,
a residue
in your mind
showing up
like an unwanted guest
to remind you.

It's too late to say,

Mom, I'm sorry.

Answering Machine

BY LYNDEE YAMSHON

I called 847-555-6033 today. I don't know why I did it. I don't know what I expected to happen. I think I was afraid of what would happen. That's why I waited so long to do it.

"Kelly isn't here. She's out with the pack. Leave your name and number and she'll call you back."

That's what her answering machine used to say. I wonder what happened to it. It was old school, the kind with an actual tape with wheels that spun. I wonder if Willy, my grandmother's boyfriend who is like a grandpa, has it in the Veterans' Home in La Jolla. I wonder if he listens to it repeatedly by pressing the button on a shaky side table next to a lumpy hospital bed. I wonder if he has the strength to reach that far or if the gangrene on his foot is eroding his leg, creeping to his hand. I wonder if he cries when he can't reach it.

I wonder if someone threw out the answering machine. I would have liked to keep it. To hear her slow, melodic voice that always sounded like a prayer appreciating things. To remind me how she just liked to sit outside on a sunny day by the pool and then later in the backyard at assisted living down the street and say, "Ohhh," as she leaned into the sun. I always had to move the heavy wired chairs so we could make a circle to fit Willy and his wheelchair, so that my family could fit to sit and chat with her after a Sunday breakfast. I would order oatmeal and orange juice and Willy would suck on prunes. My Nonnie wanted the lox and bagels, but I came so late sometimes that they'd be out. A holocaust survivor would pass out a Xeroxed copy of his story in the camps, and his little comic friend with the loud radio playing Tchaikovsky would tell me I have nice legs. Nonnie would smile and wave her hand, kind of ignoring them, but always saying a big hello at first. "I just do my thing," she'd tell us. My mother would nod. My mother does not do her own thing. Neither do I. But we are changing to be more like her.

I don't remember a time when each new telephone ring didn't

make us worry if she fell out of bed, if she was feeling okay, if Willy was dehydrated, if she was dehydrated, if she was eating enough, if she was watching *Dancing with the Stars*, if she was fighting with Willy, screaming her head off and telling him, "You're making me sick" or "I don't want more water. I'm going to throw up. Please." I guess things got so bad with the fighting that my mother gave them a yoga love prayer to say every morning to calm down, and my mom said, "Appreciate each other." I wonder if it worked.

Sometimes when the answering machine would pick up, she'd call us back, or we'd just keep calling. Sometimes we'd go in shifts, calling the nurse on duty and, if we were still getting ignored, we'd go over there. I'd go to be fun. She'd ask me to sing my originals on the guitar and she'd sway with her index fingers in the air. Or she'd ask me to turn around and would compliment my outfit. "You have such a darling figure," she'd say. My mother would go over there to scold her, like she does to her eighth graders, about picking up the phone and getting more health services. My dad would listen to her lungs and take her blood pressure. She'd pull me aside and say, "Never in my life did anyone tell me what to do."

Today I dialed 847-555-6033. It's a sunny day today, about seventy degrees, perfect for sitting around and saying, "Ohhh." I walked around all day in the sun until now, when I arrived at this café to call her answering machine. I didn't know if someone else would pick up. If I'd hear someone else's voice. I found out the number I reached was out of service.

She would have loved today.

Hey, Girlfriend

BY MARY LANGER THOMPSON

Dearest Dee,

I'm guessing from your perspective it hasn't been that long since I attended your daughter's wedding. You were the Guest of Honor, represented by a bouquet of red roses resting on a white folding chair in the front row. The wedding was outside on an Oregon hilltop. Kimberly was beautiful. She has your smile and eyes, but dark hair rather than your blonde hair. It brought back memories of when I was in your ceremony and you were in mine, forty-five years ago. Can you believe I'm sixty-eight? You would be seventy next month. Jeez, you know we had a plan to be little old ladies together.

After you died, I used to get emotional every day on the way to school in my 1969 Karmann Ghia (the car you said looked like me from the back). All the songs we used to listen to set me off, especially, "You Are So Beautiful to Me." Then one day I had heart palpitations and called my doctor, who told me to go to the nearest emergency room. There, as I lay on a cot, a young, kind doctor asked if I was under stress. I'll bet he was sorry later. I told him how I had lost my best friend to leukemia, the kind that takes you in three days. I told him we had grown up next door to each other since I was in the fifth grade and you the seventh, our bedroom windows immediately across from each other, only our side yards separating us. Remember how I used to wait for your light to come on at night, Noxzema smeared on my face, and I would whistle across to you to get news of a date?

I was better, after talking to this doctor, although there have been crazy dreams where I run after you to ask you where you've been. You can still run fast. Remember that P.E. teacher in high school that made you cry because you forgot your gym clothes? I heard they kicked her out of P.E. and made her teach English as a Second Language.

Early on, I visited your gravesite in Forest Lawn and got upset because only the years were on your stone, not the actual dates when you were born and died. When I asked how to get to your plot, the woman at the gate told me to go to the first trash can and turn right. How insensitive is that? I couldn't get over it. I wrote a poem about that. Writing has helped me cope with a lot of things in life.

After your funeral in August of 1980, your husband, Rex, sold your home and took your girls, ages six (Kimberly) and three (Karin) from California to Oregon. I was surprised to receive the letter in February saying he was remarrying already. I felt betrayed for you. Rex and Maxine married on Valentine's Day of 1981, and when I talked with Rex on what's now an old-fashioned phone, I have to admit that fate or something strange or miraculous was at work. Your replacement was an elementary teacher, like you. In fact, she was Kimberly's new first-grade teacher in Oregon, and Kimberly introduced her father to her on a hot (in more ways than one) September Back to School Night. Then, get this: her birthday is the same as yours. She was of the same religion as you and Rex, too, and although you and I had had many discussions and agreed to disagree and not talk about our different faiths, I had to admit that divine intervention or kismet or something seemed to be at work.

It was several years before Dave and I went up to Oregon to meet Maxine. I'm sorry, but I liked her. She was warm and friendly. Rex was a successful realtor and they lived in a large house with a lot of property. He took me to see the far end of their property with the swing he had hung from a tree for the girls and said, "Mary, she's a good woman, but she isn't Dee." I wonder how long it took him to notice that. I wanted to scream, "Of course not!" I knew no one could replace you fully. But I said nothing. He was still grieving. He had initially moved on but now felt stuck. I was the one who hadn't accepted things.

When Kimberly was seventeen, she wrote me a letter from Oregon. Rex had left Maxine for another woman. He was not providing support, and Maxine was adopting the girls. Maxine was not you, but she had become the girls' mother and she was very much loved by them. By that time, I loved her, too.

But then, not much later, I received a letter from Maxine. She wrote, "When one door closes, another opens." Well, that's true, but you know before you enter that second door, you have to make sure that there's a floor on the other side. However, the door that was opening was that she had begun to date your newly divorced brother, Jeff! If I didn't know better, I'd think that you were manipulating all this magnanimous behavior! Or maybe I don't know better.

To be magnanimous, to be kind and open to others, is the main lesson you taught me when we lived next door to each other. I'm still in training.

At Kimberly's wedding, I was in for more surprises. We sat at Rex's table. He came alone, and I sensed that his new woman was not yet accepted. He said, "You know who married Kimberly, don't you?" I didn't. The minister was Maxine's first husband.

The father-daughter dance with the bride made me happy, to be able to be your eyes that day. First, the bride and groom danced. Then, Kimberly and her father. Then Kimberly and the minister. Lastly, the bride and your brother, Jeff, danced. He and Maxine had tied the knot! Kimberly said, "We call him Dunkle. Dunkle, short for Dad/Uncle."

Dave and I danced, too, and Rex told us that you and he thought we'd never last! You never shared that with me. You and Rex introduced us and insisted we go out on that first date!

Rex eventually married the woman he left Maxine for. They bought a house near Maxine and Dunkle because they are all grandparents now. Yes, grandparents. Kimberly has two children, a boy and a girl. The grandparents, all four, get together to socialize and hold family councils to help their many children and their children. But we never will get over the loss of you. As you can see, everyone keeps rearranging themselves because of you. I don't think human beings ever get over this loss thing, no matter what their faith.

I know you loved history (remember the college course on the Balkans you helped me pass?), so I'll update you somewhat. People today drive everything from big huge cars to cars known as Smart Cars that are smaller than your blue VW Bug. There are even self-driving cars! Gays can currently get married in most states. Neil Diamond still sings. You'd have voted for Obama given your McGovern work, but you'd be appalled by the current campaign with its name calling and bullying on both sides. We now have a war in the Middle East instead of Vietnam (remember when Dave was writing to me from there and I first told you I loved him?). We were attacked by terrorists flying planes into the Twin Towers in New York on September 11, 2001, and now terrorists strike at any time all over the world. Civil Rights are still a huge issue. Remember the protests in 1968 at our college?

Kimberly became an elementary school teacher, too, like you, and I became a principal. I'm retired, but it was easier to be a teacher than a principal, what with a secretary who had tattoos, was a former pole dancer, and was bipolar. Charter schools are taking over our public schools and all both do is test kids and tell us how horribly our kids are doing. Standards are higher, educators are more focused, but art and music and field trips are all out the window. Some schools are so focused on testing and scores that the kids are extremely anxious, and I can see why. There are no more blackboards. Teachers have whiteboards and teach with computers. We don't use ditto masters anymore. No more stained purple hands or kids sniffing the air for the fluid that fueled the machines.

You wouldn't believe how technology has changed all our lives. I'm sure we'd be e-mailing or on something called Facebook regularly between California and Oregon if you were alive. Everyone carries a cell phone now.

Medicine is better, but even with transplants people still die of leukemia. We haven't beaten breast cancer or any other cancer entirely yet, either. And now there's a type of heart disease they call Broken Heart Syndrome.

In closing, you and I and our good friend, Camille, who turned seventy the other day, spent way too much of our time together daydreaming about being with one guy or another, instead of enjoying each other's company. I probably wouldn't be this much of a work-in-progress had you stuck around. You always pointed out the best in people I criticized. You inspired me to be more compassionate and more forgiving. I sure miss our talks. Like the cliché says, "True friends are rare." And you were the truest.

Love, and, as we used to say, "Later,"

Mary

Another Chance

BY JAMES ANTHONY ELLIS

If I were given more time with my mother, who passed in July,
2014,
I would gently hold her hand, look deeply into her eyes, and
then ask,
"Is there something you would like to say?"

I would invite her to talk about all the painful stuff we never
talked about. All those things we avoided because we
thought it wouldn't matter. Or thought would be too much
to deal with.

And then I would stay open for any words left unsaid.

I would wait. I would be patient.

And if she remained silent, I would keep still. Not needing
anything. Not demanding anything. But remaining open-
hearted and open-minded.

I would leave the space open for her to feel the safety. I would
leave the door open for her to enter.

And whether she spoke or not of those life experiences that hurt
or harmed, I would stay present with her. A son knows of
the pain of the mother. He shares it. He carries it into his
future if it is not addressed.

I faced my pain in my own healing through the years. And in
that facing of my pain, I met up with my mother's invisible
presence in the corners of my mind. I met up with her pain.
But I didn't know what to do with it. So I just left it.

Perhaps that is the right thing to do.

I didn't want to tread too harshly in areas so vulnerable and
sensitive. And because of that, I left it hidden. Even though

I believed it hurt my mother for her to keep things under wraps, I just let it be and didn't press my beliefs or demands upon her.

And so, if given another chance to be with her, I would simply let her know that I am here—open, patient, willing—to allow her to share anything that still resides within the soul, which still may cause pain and sorrow.

But it will all start with a simple question: "Is there something you would like to say?"

3rd Avenue North, Seattle

BY DONNA HILBERT

Look, Dear Heart, it's me
in winter cap and coat,
dressed, for once, for weather,
posed in front of the old apartment
where we were always cold
and often hungry. Meager haunt
of sauce-less spaghetti,
of peanut butter and day-old bread.
You were a student here, studying
into the night while I read novels
and felt abandoned and unloved.
Sundays, I bawled on the phone
to Mother and you called your dad
to talk sports, laugh about my cooking.
Here is where I lay on the sofa
aflame with fever, where a punk
intruder punched your front teeth loose.
Here is where we fought every day,
made love every night.
Here is where we brought
our first two babies home.
Here is where we mapped
our sparkling future.
Here is where we couldn't wait to flee.

Now, the babies are grown
and you, Dear Heart, are gone.
But, you would recognize this place,
it's just as we left it—
the faded paint, the splintered door
opening to the asphalt lot.

Even Then

BY DONNA HILBERT

Even in the time unhappiness
washed over me, a flood
that I was helpless to control,
when every night I dreamt of freedom
before we said our old love's dead and gone,
in the time before our new love
bloomed in joy and promise,
even then, Dear Heart,
I never wished for this.

Remembering Evelyn

BY JUDITH STRAUSS LEADER

D ear Mom,

I was asked what I would do and say if I had a few more minutes to spend with you, the real you before that dreadful dementia took over. Well, after hugging you and getting hugged back, I would want to hear your laughter. I'd enjoy hearing you tell me that I can do anything, but I'll pass on you pointing out my faults and the things I'm doing wrong. I'd love to hear your humorous take on life, and I could use some of your creative advice and problem-solving skills. Also, it would be grand to share a few adventures again in the retelling—like when you and my kid sister moved me across the country and you wouldn't let me push her into the Grand Canyon. (Five days in a car together was a bit too much closeness!) Or the time the oven broke while we were cooking Thanksgiving dinner together, as we did for twenty-five years, with you traveling to wherever I was living at the time. Remember the year we had to move the living room furniture into the bedroom to make room for all the guests?

I would want you to celebrate the adults your grandchildren have become: to hear the music Morgan creates, plays, and sings; to meet Jeanette's two beautiful sons; to chat with Reina and share her sweet wisdom and joyfulness; to play (or, more accurately, attempt to play) the interactive games Josh creates. You could joke with your sons-in-law. We'd all love to again see your smile and feel your warmth, and to have more time with all your beautiful qualities that dementia stole from you.

Mom, I want to experience you without you being angry or mean. I want to see you physically and emotionally pain-free. I want to see you feed yourself and hear you speak clearly, be understood, know that you're being understood, and respond appropriately. I want a few more minutes when you're really, really with us—like the flashes we had a few times at the nursing home—the clear, beautiful, happy you who popped in for a twenty-second visit and then disappeared.

Donna and I would be grateful for a little time for you to love us back the way you used to, before the ten agonizing years of slow deterioration of your mind and eventually your body. Before you were always irritable. Before you were always sad. Before you left us—alone, confused, angry, lost, struggling—during those last years until you were finally at peace. The years when not only did you not know us, and we didn't recognize the lady in the wheelchair, but when you lost the knowledge of the incredible person you were.

I'd like to experience the real Evelyn again—the lady with inexhaustible energy who was a talented milliner and dress designer; dedicated wartime volunteer; practicing pianist; lovely singer; beautiful bride; efficient bookkeeper; proud mother; storyteller extraordinaire; effective PTA officer, classroom mom, Girl Scout Leader; smart businesswoman working alongside Dad; barrier breaker as the first female officer on your synagogue's board of directors; middle-aged widow administering a law office and investing millions of dollars; world traveler and student; volunteer teacher of basic skills; and so much more. You were a strong, smart, caring, witty, beautiful woman admired by many.

I would make sure you know you are not forgotten and hope you somehow feel our never-ending love.

Mom, I'd remind you that your life mattered—that you made a difference!

Love always,

Judi

Discovering Truth

My mission in life is not merely
to survive,
but to thrive; and to do so with some
passion, some compassion,
some humor,
and some style.

—Maya Angelou

The Women We Were

BY CHANEL BROWN

One morning after I graduated from high school, I woke up with a panic that vibrated in jagged waves from my chest to the ends of my limbs. I was desperate not to repeat the lives of the people around me, especially the lives of the women who raised me, though I loved them. I think my mother had the same fear and wanted to help me leave, though we never talked about it. She drove me to register at the community college the same morning. Her wedding ring clinked against the glass as she flicked cigarette ashes out the window.

I moved in with Jennie that winter, and she helped get me a job at the treatment center where she worked. Jennie was my mother's AA sponsee and was between my age and my mother's, sometimes relating more to one of us than the other. She smoked Newports because she liked how they burned her throat. An older man at the treatment center told her it was because she was too green to burn. Some evenings, before my parents lost their house, Jennie and her fiancé, Billy, would come over to study the Big Book. My father would take the tone of a preacher, eager to have an audience after being raised in a family who didn't want him. When I was a teenager he would sometimes take my hand and write "Your dad loves you" in my palm. It took me some years after his death—after going through boxes of his things, pictures of him with black eyes from the 1960s in elementary school—to understand what that would have meant to him.

Jennie wore a black satin kimono from Shopko when she got up in the morning, her dyed-blonde hair falling around her face that way it does the day after it's been washed and styled. One corner of her mouth flared up, kind of like Elvis, an after-effect of having had Bell's Palsy after her first husband slammed her head into a wall. Somehow it made her more beautiful. When she took a drag, she put the cigarette to that side of her mouth, her lips reminding you a little of the King or Brando, a little masculine in contrast to her small nose, inky eyes, Marilyn Monroe hair. Her teeth were a little too big, and I loved her.

She smoked her menthol cigarettes in the morning, with a bare leg propped on a coffee table cluttered with dishes, a baby bottle, her kids' school supplies. I helped her take care of her kids and do her dishes and wanted her to love me, wanted to be like her: graceful, beautiful, in spite of everything else. She seemed always to be looking at nothing, reclining, calm in the midst of chaos. One night in December there was a snow storm. "I can't drive in the snow," she said as I handed her the keys. "It's so pretty it almost hypnotizes me."

At AA meetings she seemed to draw an audience just by being there. People were drawn to her beautiful, crooked smile and loud laugh. One night at a meeting she stabbed out half a cigarette into an ashtray. A woman emptying the trays asked her if she wanted the butt, and she waved her hand, no. "Oh, it's like that," the woman said. Jennie looked up at the woman with her cerulean eyes, lined in black, and stared at her for a moment. Then, turning away, she pulled a fresh cigarette from the green and white pack.

My only real duty on graveyard at the treatment center was to check patient rooms every half an hour. Sometimes I did homework for my classes, but it was difficult to work, sitting alone at a desk at the end of a long, white hallway. The walls started to quiver if I looked at them too long. Because we worked in the youth building, I almost got fired once for accidentally leaving a jar of instant coffee out when I left in the morning. Jennie got in trouble for wearing skirts that were too short. "What am I supposed to wear?" she asked. "A burlap sack?"

Jennie and Billy broke up, and she got a new boyfriend who bought her another car after the one we were sharing broke down. It was an old car and the steering wheel shook if you drove faster than fifty. The speed limit on the highway to the treatment center was seventy, so I drove with a steel grip on the wheel, praying I made it.

One day the tire went flat while I was at work, and Jennie's boyfriend came out to look at it. He said I must have run over something, and I said I didn't think I ran over anything, and Jennie said okay, but then later told me I should just tell her if I did something to the tire.

"I don't think I ran over anything," I said.

"Dan says you must have." Her face was hard, her jaw set. She believed Dan. A week later, I packed up my things and moved into the first apartment I ever had on my own. I lost touch with Jennie except for occasionally seeing her at work as we changed shifts.

I broke up with my boyfriend around the same time that I moved out of Jennie's, and my apartment felt like somewhere I was pretending to be an adult. After work, I drove back through the canyon road the treatment center was on, to do the dishes and find quarters for laundry. After a few months, I quit working at the treatment center and moved back in with my parents for a while, before I moved to Seattle to attend the University of Washington as a transfer student. Both of my parents died before I graduated. Jennie and I lost track of each other.

I've tried to find her through mutual acquaintances, but no one seems to know where she is. She isn't on social media, which I knew but looked for her there anyway. I wonder if she still goes to AA meetings or if she still looks the same? I wonder if in getting older she's losing some of the attention she was used to, if her spot at the table looks a little more like everyone else's? I wonder where she moved to when she married Dan, and how old her children would be now?

I wonder what is possible to take with us, and what we have to leave behind.

Waking Up

BY SIERRA RIGDON

A dull blackness leaves my head and I can feel the cool night air surrounding me. My eyes are closed, my body rocking back and forth. I'm numb from head to toe, but the pain between my thighs is razor sharp. A crushing, foreign weight is pressing down on my entire body. I open my eyes and see the silhouette of Andre on top of me, verifying my worst fear.

My throat burns. My breath is trapped there, like a wild animal trying to escape, and tears prickle the back of my eyes. In this moment, it's excruciating to exist. I'm so confused.

When did I get on the roof? Why is he doing this to me?

I slam my eyes closed. *This isn't happening. This can't be happening.* He stands, stammering, "I'm sorry. You're just so beautiful." I squeeze my eyes tighter, trying to eliminate the sound of his voice. I don't want to hear his apology. I don't want to be near him.

Almost as if he hears my thoughts, he's going back into the house through the window. I hear him mutter another quick "sorry," and he's gone. I'm left lying on the frigid, hard roof, shorts around my ankles, trying to grasp what just happened.

It was my second time doing acid. I had done it for the first time the night before and was already desperate to feel the beautiful sensations again. I loved the way my stomach had tingled, the telltale sign that the high was beginning to take over and transport me out of this reality. My close friends, Sunshine and Thomas, had also popped a double-dropped paper of LSD7 into their mouths and were already lost in their own worlds.

When we arrived at Lee's, a house we'd been taking solace in since the beginning of the summer, we immediately went upstairs to the living room and said hello to everyone. I noticed the tingling in my gut was gone; nothing was happening. I didn't want to feel sober around people who were most definitely not, so I started to get annoyed that I couldn't feel anything anymore.

"I don't feel the acid; I don't think it's working," I told Thomas, who had taken a seat next to me on the couch.

"Have you ever taken Ambien?" Horse, a friend I'd known for a couple years, asked from behind me. He must've overheard me talking to Thomas.

"No," I said, thinking back through all of the drugs I'd tried. He pulled two small pills from his pocket and handed them to me.

"Take these. If you stay awake, you'll feel high in about forty-five minutes." I gladly accepted the offer, chasing the high I was craving.

I followed a few people downstairs and watched as they started making hamburgers for dinner. I stood in the kitchen, looking for something to do. The room was dark, except for the light coming from the adjoining living room and the light above the stove. Working my way to the dirty dishes lining the sink, I passed my friend Andre. His hand grazed my arm, and he turned to me. "You're so beautiful."

"Thank you," I said, laughing off the random, rare compliment and reaching for a clean cup behind the mess.

He took a step closer and looked into my eyes. "Really, I could kiss you," he whispered, so low I almost didn't hear him. His words were unexpected. I was flattered, but also a little uncomfortable. Andre wasn't really my type. His dark eyes intimidated me. He was a fighter, a good one at that, and I'm not the type of person who likes watching violence.

"Too bad you have a girlfriend," I joked and returned to filling my glass from the faucet. I guzzled it and hurried into the living room. There were about eight people in the room. They were grouped together watching a small TV. Thomas wasn't in there. It wasn't a big deal, though. He liked being alone to fry. I wondered where Sunshine was—probably still upstairs in the recliner. I sat down on the lumpy, puke yellow 70s sofa and trained my eyes on the TV screen. I let my mind wander, experiencing the high that was just beginning.

I thought back to the first time I came to this house that had become my home. "Come on, you'll know a few people there. You'll have fun!" Cheyenne, my best friend, cajoled me as we walked out of the local concert venue. She wanted me to go to Lee's house with her, which was a twenty-five minute walk. I agreed and followed the parade of people going in that direction. The warm summer night and city lights made me feel alive.

We arrived at the house: tall and white, on the corner of a back road, completely surrounded by a three-foot-tall chain-link fence. All the lights were on, and I could hear bass bumping from inside. My stomach fluttered with apprehension. I followed Chey up the path and stone porch steps. She rapped on the door with a tight fist. It opened almost immediately and we were welcomed inside. I closed the heavy wooden door behind me.

I was amazed at what I saw. An open living and dining room, sparsely furnished, crammed with people on the couch, drinking, playing beer pong, talking, and laughing. A door opened in the back and smoke billowed out. The smell of weed and cigarettes hit me like a wall. I felt so out of place, like a sore thumb or a red nose.

Chey strode effortlessly through the house, saying hello to everyone. I stayed close and followed her to a door at the back of the kitchen that opened to a flight of stairs. Halfway down was a door that led outside, and we headed through it. We sat down together at an old, red picnic table. A potted cactus sat at the far end. Chey pulled out two cigarettes and passed one to me. I lit the Marlboro and sucked in the thick smoke like oxygen as she told me about the house and how Lee got to stay there for free, with no parental supervision, even though he was only sixteen, our age. She told me that the people who hung out there were the most carefree people I'd ever meet and said they threw a party almost every night.

Before long we were back inside, drinking and having a wonderful time. I fell in love with the house. It felt like a home I'd never had before, a family I'd always longed for. It gave me freedom, peace of mind, and the feeling that I fit in somewhere.

— — —

Last night while on the lumpy couch in the messy, smoke-filled room, I noticed that the crowd was gone and only four or five of us remained. Just then, Andre walked in holding sharpies. "Does anyone want a tribal tattoo?" he asked no one in particular. A girl I had never met before volunteered first. She got a flower on her forearm, then others asked for one, too.

I liked the way their tattoos were turning out, so when he finished, I asked him if I could have one. "Sure, come with me. I have more colors," he said, gathering his things and heading for the door. I followed him up the stairs and into a back room. He got more colors out of his bag, closed the door, and sat next to me on the bed.

"Where do you want it?" he asked.

"Right here," I said, patting the side of my leg. He began drawing an elaborate piece in neon orange that took up most of my thigh.

- - -

I stare into the night sky. The stars spin uncontrollably and make me feel like one of those cartoon characters that just got knocked out. My mind is in a fog. The last thing I can remember is Andre drawing on my leg, long deliberate strokes. I will myself to move, to no avail. Finally, I gather all the courage and strength I have and pull up my shorts.

A wave of fear crashes over me. *I need to get away.* I work my way to the open window and climb inside. The room is dark, the door closed. I stumble toward the tiny sliver of light coming from the hallway. I make my way to the kitchen, avoiding eye contact with anyone. I don't want to be questioned or have anyone see the fear in my eyes. I reach the safety of the staircase and hurry out the back door. Thankfully, no one is at the table, which is now covered with graffiti and what is left of the cactus. I run past it, around the corner to the driveway, and sit in the darkness— hoping no one will come out and see me, or, even worse, hear me cry.

I sit, weeping for what seems like an eternity. Waves of confusion, anger, fear, and disgust keep crashing into me. My body is shaking and I can't make it stop. I put my head between my knees and start taking deep breaths.

Moments later, I feel a hand on my shoulder. Thomas, his brows furrowed and his face showing what looks like years of worry, sits down next to me. "What's going on?"

I start crying again. I don't want to think about what just happened. I don't want to think about anything. Thomas persists, his voice more intense with each word. "Sierra, tell me what's going on. Are you okay?"

Shaking, sounding unfamiliar to me, a voice claws its way up

out of my throat. "I don't know. I don't know what happened."
Another wave of sobs rips though my body, leaving me feeling
helpless and overwhelmed.

"Come on," he says and pulls me to my feet. He directs me to
the door, leads me up the stairs and into Lee's room. He leaves
the light off and closes the door. He lays on the floor and pulls me
to him, cradling me in his arms. I lay my head on his chest and
cry. Knowing exactly what I need, he doesn't ask questions or tell
me everything is going to be okay. I am more than grateful he is
by my side. We eventually fall asleep this way, his shirt soaked
and black from my mascara.

The next morning, Thomas is still by my side, his protective
arm still wrapped halfway around me. I sit up, pull my fingers
through my tangled hair, and stretch. The memory of last night
invades my thoughts, raking my brain, crushing me.

I need a cigarette.

I struggle to my feet, make my way through scattered sleeping
bodies to the front porch, and climb up over the railing. I sit on
the bench and look for re-burns in the old coffee tin. I find a few
and grab a lighter from the mailbox. I light up the first one and
suck it down like water, then the next.

In the middle of an inhale, I notice the orange markings on
my leg. My heart sinks into my stomach. The smoke turns to tar
in my throat. I think I'm going to be sick. My eyes burn. I spit on
my leg and rub furiously at the snake-like image on my leg. After
a minute, there's barely any difference, but now my skin feels raw.
Panic rises in my chest. My head is spinning. *I need to get this off
right now!*

My frantic scrubbing is interrupted by the creak of the front
door. I turn to look and see Andre step out. The warm summer
morning turns chilly in an instant.

I freeze. *No. This isn't happening—this* can't *be happening.* I'm
terrified. I don't want to be near him. My heart is pounding in
my chest and in my head. He climbs the railing and plops down
next to me. "Got a smoke?" he asks, eyeing the butt between my
fingers.

"No," I say, gesturing toward the can. He searches, picking
out a few I missed, and grabs the lighter sitting between us. My
fear turns to rage.

How dare *you have the audacity to come near me, acting like
nothing happened? How dare you take away the only place I feel at*

home? This is my safe-haven! My sanctuary! How could you do that to me? I thought we were family! My head is spinning out of control. My entire body is on fire. *Family doesn't do that to each other.*

The world is spinning around me, making the shapes and colors blend together in an awful way. The air is being sucked from my lungs. I want to punch him. I want to scream at him. I want to cry and run away as fast as I can. I want to throw things and puke. I am trapped in this endless swirling chaos that is my mind.

"Hey," he says, snapping me back to my nightmare on the porch. He looks into my eyes. "I'm sorry."

I stare at him for a moment, unable to comprehend the meaning of the two words. "It's okay," I finally say.

I know I need to leave this house. Everything inside of me tells me to run. Why am I choosing this life for myself? I've seen what drugs can do to a person, their life and the lives around them. I know how much it hurts. When I was younger, I sat alone in cluttered, dark, unfamiliar rooms, waiting patiently for my mom to get her fix and to come back so we could finally go home. I watched her get escorted from our home to the back of a police car when I was in second grade. I know there is something more that I am supposed to accomplish in life and that I won't get there continuing down this path. I need to get out. I need to stop making the decisions that put me in situations like this.

I need to leave, but, at the moment, I don't have the strength. So I do the only thing I can do. I rush back into Lee's room, back to the safety of the floor and Thomas. I close my eyes, push all thoughts from my head, and try to escape by falling back to sleep.

Airport Gifts

BY ELIZABETH COPLAN

Just as the plane from Houston landed at Sea-Tac Airport, the parents of the Ometepe delegates began to congregate at the entrance to baggage claim. We discussed our excitement to see our children and the improbable possibility of catching the next ferryboat back to our own island at the end of spring break, with Friday traffic already slowed to a crawl. I stood talking with other parents about how quiet and peaceful our homes were with one of our children gone.

At the plane's scheduled arrival time, the number of anxious parents swelled. Off to the right, I noticed another group forming. They were of all ages, carrying red, white, and blue balloons, and Mylar balloons shaped as American flags. Some carried roll-up banners. Their excitement reverberated throughout the waiting area. They exuded an energy of relief, mixed with giddiness and held-back tears.

And then they saw the soldiers walking down Concourse B and toward the waiting group. One solider, a young man, looked somber in expression but proud in his uniform. At his side, the other soldier was older and weary-looking, but also somber, also proud. Then the frenzy of their welcoming party climaxed as the children shouted their names and the tears were held back no longer. One boy opened his banner: Welcome Home, Uncle Joe!

Without slowing his pace, the younger soldier went to his wife, gave her a quick kiss, then fell into a long embrace—a desperate, I'll-never-leave-you-again-if-I-can-help-it embrace.

Minutes ticked by, but time seemed to stop. The baby in the stroller began to cry. The soldier scooped up the child and held him close in one arm, his other arm around his wife's waist as she put her head on his chest. Not a word was said. The baby choked back sobs while he studied the face of this man holding him.

I turned away, sensing that the moment was too private. My gaze turned momentarily to the older soldier, who held a man and a woman close to him—a brother and his wife or his parents?

No one spoke. Clearly words don't come easily at a homecoming such as this one. What do you say to someone who has seen too much and has experienced the unimaginable, traumatic events of war?

The frenzied anticipation of the crowd gradually gave way to measured interaction. Other family members came forward for their turn to show their love for the returning soldiers. I wanted to add my "thank you." I wanted to surround them with a protective light that would keep them from harm. They had come so far, but now they were home again.

When I saw my son walking toward me, I still felt the combination of love and sadness from the soldiers and their families. My own son did not look particularly excited to see me. I am sure I represented the end of his amazing journey.

He had a new family now, one in a tiny village on Ometepe in Nicaragua. During the past two weeks, he'd witnessed a birth and dug fence pole holes with sticks that only remotely resembled shovels. He'd built piñatas and entertained village children. He'd climbed a volcano, fought off colonies of ants, eaten rice and beans at every meal. He'd lived in a shack without water or electricity. He'd seen the smiling faces of children with so little and yet so much. I'm certain he was glad to be home but could not wait to go back.

I started to cry, but they were not tears for Spencer. They were for other mothers' children, who went off to war, experienced debilitating disease or illness, remained uneducated, starved, or died. I closed my eyes and sent my motherly love to these children of the world. In doing so, I realized that I was standing at the happiest place on earth.

Alone

BY TERRY SEVERHILL

I've lost him.
And I'll never be the same.
It hurts
Deep
And lasting.
I cannot or maybe it's just I will not shed tears.
My body won't cry,
My mind weeps,
Alone,
And unheard.
We met in the middle of a far-off country
In the middle of a war
In the middle of nowhere,
In the middle of forever.
We traded futures,
Laughed at our pasts.
I buried them last night.
Our dreams mingled with memories.
He was back from the war just eight months.
He'd lost his dreams and had forgotten the past.
He shot himself.
All alone.

He Didn't Die with Death

BY SHERYL BURPEE DLUGINSKI

Grief is not always the result of death. At eight years old I lost my father, but he didn't die. In that same moment, I lost myself too. It would take fifteen years for me to begin to find myself again. If I could return to that fateful time now, here is what I would say to my father:

"Please, don't do this. You are very drunk and may not even remember this tomorrow. I will forget, too, for many years, tucking these memories away in the creases of my brain, hoping to bury them forever. But these memories will refuse to stay hidden. They will rot and fester in the folds between my ganglia, telling me I am damaged, forsaken, unlovable.

"Look at me, Dad. See the person I am—a small girl aching for your love, affection, and attention; needing your guidance, wisdom, and experience. I love you. I need you to be my father, not my predator. Please stop. Now. Before you blow shrapnel of confusion, pain, and guilt through my heart, lodging it there until I can gather the courage to extract and examine each jagged, smoldering piece."

And here is what I would say to my innocent child self, lost forever in the putrid darkness that night:

"Please don't go, little one. Stay and fight. Scream, cry, say no. This is not love. No matter what he tells you. You are not meant to be his source of comfort. No. The truth is very much the opposite. It is his job to comfort you. And though it's sad beyond reason that he is incapable of real love, please don't accept this distorted facsimile as genuine.

"You thought you could finally win his ever-elusive love and approval. You thought this would make you the special one. You didn't understand that giving up your eight-year-old body—so thin, he joked you looked like a refugee of war—and keeping his filthy secret, in return for his twisted version of love, was no bargain. How could a third grader see that his heart was too crippled to give you the unconditional love that was your birthright? I see now why you had to burrow so deep and far from the world that you suffocated yourself. I understand you hid yourself to keep safe, alive, and sane until you might be unearthed. Now that you've been resurrected, each day I breathe a bit more life back into you. I'm sorry you had to keep that secret for so long. Thank you, brave spirit, for allowing us to heal and become whole again."

Angry

BY EMILIE WINTHROP

I'm so mad at you I could sock you in the nose. How could you go off and leave me like that? I am paralyzed without you. I can't sleep. My eyes are so swollen from crying I can't even go out in public, much less work. I can't eat or do much of anything.

You didn't work enough, so they tell me I won't get much Social Security and I'm still too young to put in for mine. When the rent comes due, I'll either have to get the landlord to trust me till my next paycheck, or maybe he'll chuck me out onto the street. I can hardly afford food, so maybe it's a good thing I don't feel like eating. You were supposed to be here to help with the bills, help pay the rent, and help me.

Even when I'm livid at you, I miss you. I need to feel your arms around me again. I want you here to kid me: tell me I'm too thin, or too fat, tell me I'm a lousy cook. I need to hear you whisper, "I love you." I need to kiss your handsome face and feel your breath on my cheek. I ache for you.

If we'd had kids, maybe they'd be able to help their old mother, but, no, you didn't want to "bring them into this rotten world." It's rotten, all right, when someone you love just up and shoots himself and leaves you behind.

~~Dear Dad~~

BY JOSH SALMON

~~Dear Dad~~

Dear Shane,

The basement was, to me, the void. The void was your space. The empty part of the house set aside for the non-caring parent. Your carpet downstairs, gray and uncomfortable, the huge TV that I couldn't use, unless I was watching TV with you. I couldn't be in the void unless there was something that you wanted me to do. We didn't sit down to have personal talks, man to man. It makes sense now how I didn't even know that my aunt had her baby girl till I saw her at your family camping trip. I know more about my uncles on Mom's side than about your whole family combined.

If you're reading this, then our relationship has come to its end. I don't regret that it's over. I wonder—do you? I gave you plenty of space and time to be part of my life, but you threw it away. I wanted to have a relationship. I guess you didn't.

Do you remember the first time we had a real hard-core argument, both of us angry and frustrated? It was about your damned chips. I was eight years old. You came home at 7:00 p.m. Mom made dinner even though you had already eaten. No "Hi" or "How's it going?" Just like every day. Only you storming up the stairs and down the hall toward my room. I turned off my TV and games because I knew you were pissed for some reason. You burst into my room, your face so red I swear that your head was going to explode, holding out the empty chip bag.

"What's the matter?" I asked.

"Did you eat my chips?"

"I had one bowl," I replied.

"Don't you ever eat my chips! When you have money to buy chips, then you can eat them!"

The funny part was that it wasn't even your money that bought the chips. I had helped Mom put the groceries away on Monday. I knew you didn't buy them because you didn't share bank accounts with anyone. Later that day, I saw you grab them from the pantry and take them downstairs to the void. Do you know how long I went without eating any chips from your house? It was three months. I was afraid of accidently eating *your* chips. What did you stand to lose by sharing food with your kid?

I was in a sixth grade play, *The Lion, the Witch, and the Wardrobe*. I played Mr. Beaver. My costume was a brown shirt and pants with a big old beaver tail and teeth. It was nerve-racking, and I was hoping to see your face. You didn't even show up. You didn't care enough to even let it show on your radar. You didn't know how badly I was hurt; I knew you wouldn't care. If it wasn't hockey, it didn't matter. When we showed you the DVD version Mom had bought, you slept through it. I ran upstairs crying, but you didn't notice. You slept till morning, completely forgetting what you'd been doing the night before.

You told me that if I got good grades, you would show up to the things I did that were school-related. I was a solid 4.0 student, the highest grade my elementary school gave out. I did that so we could talk and so that you would show up to my events. You never did. You didn't care then and you wouldn't care now.

You told so many lies to me while I was growing up. You told me that no matter what happened when you and Mom divorced, you wouldn't do what your dad did to you: abandon me. You couldn't even keep that in mind while you were hurrying to marry that new wife of yours. The hardest part of that for me was the fact that you, my father, didn't have the guts to tell me that you were even seeing someone. My cousins and your brother knew more about what you were doing than your own child. That's no way for a kid to live. I have wondered my whole life if you were lying to me when you told me things. Did it pay out? Was it worth it? I don't think so.

Your Ex-Son,

Josh

Breaking My Silence
(Among Other Things)

BY JENNIFER D. MUNRO

I wanted to hop in the sack, but I got the sack, instead. Dark and lusty romance novel heroes go to great lengths to corrupt innocent heroines, but my boyfriends all split as soon as they heard that they would be my "first." I had passed the legal age limit for drinking and voting, so my dates didn't think they had an intact hymen to contend with. I think my potty mouth fooled them; how could a girl who talked a foul blue streak *not* have rolled in the gutter? I was anxious to discard the nun's habit of chastity, but my beaux hightailed it as soon as they learned that sex with me would have actual significance. They thought they heard the knell of wedding chimes, but I just wanted them to ring my bell. How hard could it be (very, I hoped)? I wasn't asking for an orgasm, even. Just a handy tool to knock down my last barricade to adult wisdom.

No moral code kept me unsullied all those years. I subscribed to no religion. What can I say? I got my nose stuck in a book and adolescence passed me by. I'd tarnish my virtue later. Just let me finish this chapter first. But like any Jane Austen heroine, I sensed time ticking. Time to retire the library card and check out real life experience before I became the bitter, sex-deprived witch of fairy tales. As I began my senior year of college, I decided that I would lower my drawbridge for the first decent Lancelot who knocked with raised spear. I couldn't possibly be saddled with my maidenhead when I was handed my bachelor's degree. Even my mother in the fifties had gotten the dirty deed over with before starting college (my brother being one result).

I had no trouble finding prospective candidates. A parade of knights had been there all along while I'd been dog-earing pages instead of howling at the moon. Sure, I could have had a one-night stand with a stranger. But I was enough of a romantic that

I wanted my first lover to remember my name in the morning. I wanted us to feel each other out before he felt me up. Like getting lost in the world of a good book, hooked from page one to denouement, I fell in love with each of these boys as we dated and danced our way towards the dirty deed. But while books involved a climax, my love life didn't.

Stud chose me as his bad girl on the side. A born-again Christian, Stud wrestled with memories of pre-conversion pleasures. Officially he dated Prim, a proper woman of faith. For me, Stud revealed his dark side, teaching me fancy Top Ramen recipes, advising me to eat the core along with the apple, and discussing U2 lyrics as if they were Leviticus. Stud and I skipped rapidly down the path toward fornication, until he leaned over at a party and snorted white stuff up his nostrils. He'd thought I'd been around the block a few times and would join him for a few lines before we rolled in the hay. When it turned out that I was as pure as the snow up his nose, he took off. If he was going to have to be delicate with a virgin, it would at least be one who earned him some celestial points, not another black mark against his afterlife. He went back to Prim, praying I wouldn't tell her that he got lit on more than altar candles. Poor Stud got it all backwards. Prim had lost hers a long time ago on more than tampons and horseback riding. Like many a fictional heroine, I was completely misunderstood, and the bad prince trotted off with the wrong wench.

Mustache was a good bet for my second try since he read me Emily Dickinson poetry late into the night. With his obsession for maid-to-the-grave (or was she?) Emily, his potential kink for virgins was made to order. Stud was a real looker (although I'm gleeful to note that premature balding had already begun to rear its ugly head), but maybe I'd have better luck with the average-looking Mustache. Intending to become a sports medicine doctor, he was passionate about the creak in my knees, and we groped our way toward eventual copulation. Mustache had also accepted Jesus after experimenting with most forms of deviancy during a stint in the armed forces. I was obviously attracted to the conflicted misery of these soul-searching boys, tormented by wavering faith and bad eighties hair, but I'd waited too long. My potential paramours had already tried everything (except me), and were ready to cool off while my teakettle had just started to whistle.

One night Mustache learned that he'd flunked his pre-med exam. He guzzled a bottle of expensive Russian vodka that he'd been saving—for what, I'm not sure, but failure obviously qualified. Then he unceremoniously maneuvered into blow job position. I said that's not where I wanted it, because I had this other nagging thing I needed to get rid of. Mustache ricocheted off of me and hit the wall on the other side of the room like I'd said I had V.D., not Virginity. At that point, Mustache confessed that he had a wife. I was another cross that he could not bear. God had set me in his path to keep him from crossing back to the dark side, and I should get me back to the nunnery.

Near as I can figure it, the problem with Pasty was that he was still a virgin, too. Nice guy. We hung out for a while, scuffing our toes in the dirt of first base, each waiting for the other one to steal second. Neither one of us made a move. Around the seventh inning stretch, we shook hands like good sports and left the field. We'd both try to hit a home run with someone else.

Hairy was at least honest. He said he simply didn't want the baggage of being my first. His first time had been a disaster, and he didn't want that potential weight hanging around his karma. He said I should go have bad sex with somebody else. He at least gave me an orgasm for the road. "Put it in the bank," he said. "You'll need it."

Eve sure had it easy. Temptation was nowhere in sight, until I met a man with a real live snake. I chose a scientist, figuring God wouldn't be nipping at his heels. Geek adored his cold-blooded pet. But after I watched a live mouse go down the reptile's gullet, right next to the bed, I reevaluated my immediate need for a serpent in my life and sssaid sssayonara.

So I graduated with a near perfect GPA and an illiterate G-spot. I entered the job market *cum laude* with a lonely yoni. Then my girlfriend and I took a long-planned vacation to a U.S. Naval base in Japan, where her father was stationed. I thought I would be traipsing around temples rubbing Buddhas, but I ended up rubbing shoulders with hundreds of scared and lonely sailors—many barely out of high school—about to set sail for the Persian Gulf. We were the only white, civilian women for barb-wired miles. The proper local women wouldn't give the sailors the time of day. Who was I to withhold consolation? We flicked our Bics and sang to Bon Jovi at the enlisted man's club, where six more pink *frou frou* drinks arrived in front of me before I finished my first. I wore a white Laura Ashley dress. I was treated like a Lady, and my garden needed tending. Desperation on all sides crept beneath the alcoholic hilarity, but the fact remained that I had my pick of boys who were ready, willing, and able to deflower me. There was something fitting to the pall cast over this momentous moment by the specter of war, loneliness, tragedy, and young lives squandered, both here and back home.

I chose a lovely, kind boy who pawned his watch in exchange for a guitar so he could serenade me on the streets of Yokusuka. On a romantic date, he slew my dragons of doubt by facing down a meal of raw fish to impress me. We scraped and borrowed money to rent a by-the-hour room for the night in the Love Motel with a miniature Statue of Liberty on the roof. The coincidental metaphor didn't escape me. When it was over, Lovely Boy asked me how I felt. "Relieved," I answered. He was hoping for something more profound, but for me, the moment couldn't have been deeper. More than a fleeting rite of passage that had never much interested me, it satisfied a yearning to live life fully, to connect, before chance and ill luck severed possibility. Before his ship sailed for a hostile region, he gave me his dog tag, souvenir of the night he barked up my tree.

Then, back home, I slowly and unexpectedly fell in love with a man I originally ignored. Less than a year later, I married him. The first time we slept together was no fairy tale moment: turns out our nearly thirty-year romance defines the real fairy tale.

Yet all these years later I find the tardy loss of my virginity to be my dirtiest secret. Amongst intimate and casual friends alike who divulge sordid details of affairs, abortions, same-sex experiments, shoplifting, cross-dressing, sleeping with their therapists, putting recyclables in with the trash, and forgetting the boss's time-sensitive FedEx package in the restroom, I find my long-intact hymen and lifelong monogamy impossible to confess. I feel actual shame in my lack of sexual congress until I nearly hit the quarter century mark. It's like I wet the bed, not that I kept my virginity until I had almost surpassed the lifespan of linoleum.

My current friends and acquaintances are deluded about my past experience. I've earned a reputation by proxy, as an erotica writer, gutter talker, motorcycle mama, and hip-flask bearer. Even my mother thinks I lost it long before I did. I have no excuse. Long after the Age of Aquarius set us free, I was still treading water. I came of age in the wild and carefree eighties, when the eye-shadowed boys of Duran Duran hung off the side of a speeding yacht without life preservers. Sexual barriers had all been broken. We had The Pill, and AIDS was just a rumor. And there I was, playing the French Horn and reading *The Iliad.*

I was not a God-fearing woman, living a church-prescribed choice of virginity until marriage. Sex was simply irrelevant to who I was as a person. The hymen, after all, is just a mucous membrane. Perhaps I intuited that a cultural mythology involving mucous was not worth getting uptight about and was also about as arousing as the Michael Jackson-Lisa Marie Presley kiss. Or perhaps I intuited that my technical virginity was the least of what I had to lose. With sexual knowledge came firsthand experience of a complicated world that I would have preferred to keep as fiction between the pages of a book—a novel that I could close when the plot got too intense.

Shortly before my wedding, I got the news that Pasty, the sweet boy who couldn't screw up the courage to put the moves on me, had hung himself. Instead of remembering him swinging from the rafters of his garage, I choose to remember him as he was on our carefree drive to the coast in his convertible Karmann Ghia, top down, his badly-cut mop of brown hair flying straight up in the wind, the pair of us innocent virgins, happy, with everything in the world left to lose.

Too Early Too Late

BY BETH RAHE BALAS

Dancing Jack, thirty three years
Since you tried to hijack my wedding.
I was, surprise! The One
Not your new wife, back in Virginia.

Come back, Jack.
I've aged, grown thick.
While you still tower, young
Beaming long golden waves, laughing,
"Let's dance on our toes, now..."

Oh, me in the sun, tending tomatoes, drawing.
You baking, your goats out back.
At night, though, watching me in my room next door.
I didn't know, so long ago

You said you were wrong to leave, now's our time.
But Jack, you can't fight cancer with carrots.
You were just too late all around.

Still, on a cold night of warm breath
In your dinged up yellow Toyota
You spoke so urgently of touching souls,
Of lightness, our spirits floating upwards.

For that
you were far too early.
I reach up now, searching,
Blinded by light.

Always With Me

*What we have once enjoyed we can
never lose. All that we love deeply
becomes a part of us.*

—Helen Keller

Tucked In

BY ANDREA ADAMS

It was my grandmother who tutored me, a dainty child of rumpled hippies, in the fine art of housekeeping. My parents, adrift in dust bunnies, were busy sitting on lumpy cushions swathed in musty Indian fabric while chanting for enlightenment. I cherished the lessons Grandmother provided in all things domestic, especially the proper making of a bed.

"You can take down the pillowcases," Grandmother said, smiling at me over the clothesline in her backyard. "Make sure you put the clothespins in the white bag, because they are for light-colored fabric. The denim bag has clothespins for dark-colored fabric." This made sense to me. I happily followed directions, listening to chatter from the well-tended bird feeders outside her kitchen windows.

After we brought in the baskets of laundry, we steamed and ironed the fresh linens, one piece at a time, on Grandmother's ironing board. It was set up in the kitchen, with an elaborate wire and spring to keep the cord out of the way. The floor gleamed, so there was not a worry when I dropped one of the pillowcases. I felt special, the oldest grandchild, worthy of learning how to create these incomparable beds. Her tender brown eyes hugged me with every glance, her face still smooth and beautiful, her bunion-feet in comfort shoes. The dishwasher chugged along companionably. We talked quietly, working together while Grandpa Doc saw patients in the front rooms of the house.

Upstairs in the bedrooms, she showed me how to make a deluxe cocoon of blankets and crisp, ironed sheets. Her songbird voice reached the center of my heart, and I wanted nothing more than to master this task from my very own fairy godmother. Grandma Erma. On top of the velvety cotton sheets, we'd place a spotless cotton blanket and follow that with a brawny Hudson Bay blanket made of thick white wool. It took all my strength to hold its hefty bulk, but I so admired the fat stripes of red, green, yellow, and black. Next we snapped a white, puckered seersucker sheet over the top. "Now, Dea, watch this carefully. This is how we keep all the layers secured together."

Her gnarled, arthritic hands and my small ones pulled the edge of a white, seersucker sheet up and over the top of the stack of blankets. Her soft grey curls brushed close to my nose and had a bit of a talcum powder scent. I noticed how good it felt that every single person and object at my grandparents' house was treated respectfully.

Finally, we folded the pink rose border of the ironed top sheet down, enveloping the crinkled seersucker package so that the blankets were completely invisible. "This is how you tuck in the corners so they stay tidy," said my grandmother, a former physics professor.

When visiting my grandparents, I'd come to this marvelous bed after bathing in a bathroom that was fresh and scented with bay. Sometimes there would be a dozen of us at my grandparents' house. Even so, when I was little, she'd be in the bathroom with me, scrubbing my back and wrapping me in a pink-striped towel. The old radiator often squeaked. The floor would be smooth and cool as I walked across the hall to the bedroom.

In the tightly made bed, I'd wiggle my toes down, feeling swaddled by the silky, fluid sheets against my skin. Sun-drenched wool kept me warm and cozy but was never scratchy, because it was completely wrapped in the white, puckered seersucker sheet. Summer roses seemed to permeate the blankets, leaving a waft of scent in the air throughout the year. There was often a temptation to fall asleep at once. Yet I preferred to luxuriate in the safety of the fresh, joyful shelter of my grandparents' home.

Tucked up in bed, I'd eye the delicate music box on the nightstand, wind the key, and listen to it ping the melody to *Blue Danube*. And then choose to read *National Velvet* or *Charlotte's Web* from the wood-and-glass bookshelf in the corner.

In the summer, the windows would be open just a little to let in the cool air, which made the beds all the more delicious. In the colder seasons, the windows were tightly closed, with the blinds turned down to help that large Victorian house stay as cozy as possible.

Fifty years later, I still relish the ritual of making my bed. I am gentle with a treasured, threadbare, seersucker sheet that used to be at my grandparents' house. That sheet had been the keepsake I wanted when the Hummels, chess sets, and books were distributed to family members after Grandmother died. I believed it irreplaceable. Then one day I was flipping through a fine linen catalogue and spotted "retro" seersucker sheets for sale. Before a single thing could distract me, I pulled out my credit card. Nearly dancing a jig, I ordered a white one. My grandparents, great proponents of the Sears catalogue, would have choked to see the cost. But to me this seersucker sheet was priceless.

The beds I make today can never be quite as wonderfully smooth and scented as my grandmother's. If I hung my sheets on the line here in Seattle, instead of smelling like upstate New York fresh-mown grass, they'd get rained on and spattered with mud, and I don't iron cotton sheets to a glossy sheen the way my grandmother did, either. However, I do still layer, stack, wrap, and tuck.

They Scurry About

BY TERRY SEVERHILL

Clean the plates,
cups and tableware.
They come head to head
exchanging whispers, glances,
a brief hug, a nod of approval
or a tsk, tsk, a small
head shake of disapproval.

Counter parts
scurry about
intent on their own mission
cleaning the detritus,
crumbs of the wake food.
They come head to head
exchanging pheromones
feelers/antennas rubbing each other
shifting this way or that
a dance in miniature.

Both teams reluctant
to declare everything finished.
Formicidae and Sisterus padre domesticus
each on an important mission,

tidying things up.

Trying to bring order to helter skelter,

the world left behind.

Cards and Letters

BY LORI DAVILA

While cleaning out your house, I found a very old letter you wrote to Nana after Popop died. You were an eighteen-year-old boy, in Germany, and you were writing next to a candle you lit for Popop.

I would like very much to see you through this and also to hold my mother's arm. I'm still so easy to tears. I see how important family is and I feel badly not being home now.

I was simply amazed at your beautiful, expressive prose because you were undemonstrative throughout most of your adult life. After attending four different colleges and obtaining a philosophy degree, you set out for California, thousands of miles away from your east coast family. You became more and more private about your life and you never married or had children. I assumed family became a low priority for you. Over the years we cared about each other, but we didn't talk much except when we managed Mom's healthcare and estate. I wonder why you kept your life so secretive? I wish you could write me a letter and tell me.

I cherish one rare story you did share during the last year of your life. We were gorging ourselves at a German *hofbrauhaus* after you had a full day of chemotherapy and blood transfusion treatments. I was delighted to hear your story even though it entailed hitchhiking in Germany and a man picking you up and putting his hand on your leg. I was mesmerized by your tale, more so because you were annihilating a gigantic roasted turkey leg. Your appetite had been nonexistent and you had already dropped forty pounds from the pancreatic cancer.

Deep down, you were the most sensitive one in our family. Your early letters prove it. The way you cried more than anyone else when Mom and Dad died proves it. The words you said to me on your deathbed when I was helping you eat a little bit proves it: "Your mother would be proud."

Now that you're gone, the life you kept so private and my

life are colliding. I learned that you raised two girls of a different race who think of you as their father. They are the daughters of your old girlfriend. I heard that this family moved in with you over twenty years ago and then left several years later. You never shared about the beautiful, loving relationship you had with them throughout their lives.

When we cleaned out your house, I was determined to find a keepsake that would be the essence of you. In the midst of all the philosophy books and electronic and computer parts, I found a beautiful Father's Day card from your secret family.

You have been an angel for all of us... I love everything you do... thank you for loving me...

They were some of the most beautiful sentiments I had ever read, aside from your letter to Nana. I now know you did not live your life in vain and that you had so much love in your life from this very unique family unit. I am finally getting to know all about you through my relationship with them. I only wish you allowed me to be a part of their lives sooner.

I am watching over your beautiful girls, who miss you so much. And in loving them, I am loving you, just as I always have.

This Side of Here

BY JENNIFER COATES

Water tastes soft
sweeter
as I stand where
you were last
and sip
from a fluted glass
found at your
round kitchen table
where so much happened
over wine, glazed pork
busy forks, fruit

the room
could hardly contain
the voices all speaking
at once
—you, your laughter,
the reason everyone stayed
well beyond late.

I savor it in drops
on my tongue
as if for the first
and last time
—a burst of all things
I have ever felt or tasted
now new
in this moment

like memories of you
I want to quick
yank out of
the vast velvet
dark
I can't touch,
back into the light
where I can hold you
in my hands
still warm.

Tariq

BY AZIM KHAMISA

As the twenty-first anniversary of your tragic death is approaching this month, you are particularly in my heart, thoughts, and prayers. More so as I am writing this letter in Vancouver—the city in which you were born and, sadly, buried. So the energy around this time is palpable and bittersweet. Your death was sudden, senseless, and utterly devastating.

You were a bright student at San Diego State University, with the future ahead of you. You were working that night delivering pizzas, when a young boy, a child, really, approached and shot you dead. It was part of a gang initiation called "Jacking the Pizza Man." The boy was fourteen years old. You were twenty years old. Both of your futures ended in that moment. And I thought mine had as well.

Losing you felt like the end of my own life. While I had navigated through many challenges in my life—immigrating to the United States from Kenya, the ups and downs in business, a divorce, and other transitions—this was the one challenge that completely consumed me. I had no tools to deal with the tragedy, and in my utter devastation I did not want to live anymore without you.

However, in deep tragedies sometimes there is a spark of clarity—the much talked about "dark night of the soul." Indeed this experience was that for me. The pain was so excruciating that I clearly remember leaving my body when I got the horrible news. I could not remain in my body and bear the pain. This was my first out-of-body experience, and, as a believer in God, I went into His loving arms, where He held me in a long embrace. When the explosion subsided, He sent me back into my body with the wisdom that "there are victims on both ends of the gun." That was the spark of clarity that changed the trajectory of the rest of my life.

Seeing your assailant as a victim, I approached the boy's family. I met Ples Felix, the boy's grandfather and guardian, and asked him to join me in stopping children from killing children. I said, "We've both lost our sons, my son to murder, and yours to prison."

Nine months after you were shot, I started The Tariq Khamisa Foundation. Ples continues to work with me toward our mission of breaking the cycle of youth violence. For twenty years TFK has been working to save the lives of children, empowering children in making the right choices, and teaching the principles of nonviolence.

You always wanted to do something big and change the world. TKF is doing exactly that and continues to honor your dream. Soon after starting TKF, I paid a visit to the boy who shot you, Tony, in prison. Tony, now thirty-five, will join Ples and me at TFK in 2018 when he is finally released. He is twelve units away from a degree in Child Psychology, reads five books a month, and wrote the foreword to my fourth book. We saved him, but he will save many more when he is onstage speaking with his grandfather and me.

As I look back at the last twenty-one years, I am amazed by all the work that has been done in your name all over the world. TFK has been successful in keeping kids away from gangs, violence, drugs, and alcohol. CANEI (Constant and Never Ending Improvement), an intervention program in its fourteenth year, is now in nine cities, transforming seventy percent of the youth offenders. We have reached over a million kids with live presentations. Many more million young and old people have been transformed, via substantial media coverage and a busy speaking schedule that has allowed me to present 550 keynotes worldwide.

Tariq, you put me on my spiritual mission. The work over the last twenty-plus years has been very meaningful and fulfilling. I miss you dearly and think of you several times a day. I am most grateful to you for inspiring this work. Not that I don't want you back in a New York minute, but this work is being done because of you. Know I love you dearly—thank you for changing the world.

Channelling With Grandma

BY DIANA RAAB, PH.D.

I did something different this morning—
Birdie, the psychic
told me to talk with Grandma
dead already more than four decades,
just make an appointment she said,
talk to her ask her what you like.

When everyone was sound asleep,
I plopped on your brown velour love seat,
wrapped myself in a warm robe
sat Indian style and called your name.
We have an appointment; let's talk, I whispered
as your skeleton stood before me
on the puffiest of white clouds
your arms stretched in my direction
wanting to hold but no longer knowing how.

I cried and told you
I missed you ever since
that day the ambulance drivers took you away
down those creaky wooden stairs
up my quiet childhood street
wet tears followed by dry ones
not wanting my own mother
to be nurtured by my grief, your substance.

You apologized
how I found you lying there
on Labor Day weekend,
sleeping pills spilled upon the bedside

sheer curtains swaying as birds chirp outside.

You told me you had no choice
your childhood misery strangled you.

You asked if I remembered
the long walk the night before
in our shared neighborhood
which I used to call home
where houses lined up
engulfed by well-watered gardens

When we got home
you told me you left me a gift
hidden in your walk-in closet
because I am the appointed family writer,
you knew from my very first push into the world
and my keen awareness
and hours spent seated
in my own closet
with my journal and pen
chronicling my lost world.

The gift—your very own journal
depicting our parallel lives
strongly convening
on the written page
intense and laden with emotion—
two survivors, rising after each fall
so many times
writing about what happened behind closed doors
like the one you killed yourself behind.

The Gift

BY DIANA RAAB, PH.D.

After you were gone, there wasn't much talk about you, your life, or your ending, until one day more than twenty years later when my parents were moving from Queens, New York. While packing, they stumbled upon your retrospective journal, which you'd written after emigrating from Vienna in the early 1930s. Only after reading the document did I come to understand the deep roots of your depression, which had clearly tormented you for your entire life, and eventually led to your suicide.

I tucked the journal away, and ten years later pulled it out, just after my breast-cancer diagnosis. I was hungry for answers about my illness—after all, no one in my family had ever been diagnosed with the disease. I considered the possibility that you'd committed suicide as the result of a cancer diagnosis that you'd kept to yourself. I hoped your written words could provide an explanation for my own health crisis, but they didn't. However, something even more profound occurred: the details of your tragic life drew me closer to your spirit. I also realized that my love for writing came from you, and for this I'd like to now thank you.

From your journal, I learned that you were orphaned during World War I at the age of twelve. While disturbingly unsympathetic soldiers marched through your childhood town, you witnessed Russians killing a little boy on your street. You wrote about trekking for hours through the countryside to an infirmary to find your mother dying of cholera. On a floor lined with bodies, you had to identify the one belonging to your mother. At the age of fourteen, along with your younger sister, you immigrated to Vienna and lived in an orphanage. With no parents to support you, you were forced to work in a bank while attending school.

While reading your journal, I realized that I'd never connected with another woman in the same way since your death. As a child, I was an extension of you, and even more so as an adult after your passing. I am also a survivor, having endured two different bouts with cancer, but the genetic connection I was seeking pales in comparison to the bond we share through writing. You were the person who planted the seeds for my writing—not only because you were devoted to the written word yourself (evidenced by daily journaling and a propensity for leaving notes on the kitchen table), but also because it was you who taught me how to type. The black Remington typewriter (which I now have a replica of in my own writing studio) was perched on your vanity in your bedroom. Do you remember that Saturday morning before breakfast when you invited me into your room?

The conversation went like this:

"Have a seat," you said, pointing to your vanity chair. "I'm going to teach you how to type. This is a handy skill for a girl to have, plus you never know what kind of stories you'll have to tell one day."

You stood behind me, and I gazed at your reflection in the mirror—your dark roots framing your bleached-blonde hair, and your glowing smile revealing the rather large space between your two front teeth. I wasn't surprised to learn years later that as a young woman you'd won numerous beauty contests in your native Vienna.

You took my right hand and positioned it on the home keys, carefully placing one finger at a time on each letter, repeating the same gesture with my left hand.

"This is the position your fingers should be in. When you become a good typist, you won't have to look at the letters. Let's see if we can type your name," you continued.

With my left middle finger, you had me press on the "D." Then we moved to the right middle finger and moved up a row to type an "I." Then my left pinkie pressed the "A," a tricky maneuver for a novice typist. You then instructed me to move my right thumb down to the bottom row to type an "N." Then my left pinkie typed the final "A." I glanced up at the paper to see the results of my efforts, and then proudly looked up at your face in the mirror.

"You see? You did it!" you exclaimed, squeezing my shoulders. "Like anything in life, the more you practice, the better you'll become. You must work hard to get results; you'll learn that soon enough, my love."

That moment in time marked my own lifelong commitment to writing. Days after learning how to type, I went back and forth between writing stories in my journal and typing on your Remington, much in the same way I do today—alternating from journal to keyboard. Thanks to you, in college I earned extra money by typing term papers for other students, and as a young mother I chronicled my kids' early years. As a breast-cancer survivor, I wrote a memoir based on that experience. And I completed *Regina's Closet: Finding My Grandmother's Secret Journal,* on what would have been your 100th birthday.

Although you chose to finally give up after a life spent in hardship, your life story was one that you felt compelled to share in your journal. I'm grateful for this gesture and am relieved that you chose to keep it tucked away in your closet, since you could have just as easily destroyed it. Had you done so, I would never have found it, and telling your story would not have been possible.

Writing about and studying your life has been my way of keeping you alive. Sharing your story has also allowed me to understand who you were, what you went through, our common traits, and why you ended your life. Reading your journal reminded me of the intrinsic value of writing and the value of passing on stories from one generation to the next. I believe that we stand on the shoulders of giants, but if we didn't know their stories, we wouldn't be aware of that. Your journal was the greatest gift you could have ever bestowed on me. Your words and life experiences have inspired my own writing and will continue to do so, as I hope my own words will for future generations.

Last Moments

We understand death for the first time when he puts his hand upon one whom we love.

—Madame De Stael

My Grandmother's Funeral

BY KRISTIN BRYANT RAJAN

My husband, two children, and I make the trip
from Atlanta, Georgia, to Southeastern Virginia
where my grandmother Glenelle lives
as we do every year at Christmas,
when we pile into the car with dogs and gifts
and grumbles of
"Too many suitcases—
what were you thinking?"
while loading and unloading the car.

But this time it's not Christmas:
it's mid-October.
And this time we don't drive:
we fly,
because we need to get there fast,
because funerals don't wait,
because we didn't plan on this,
because it's the only thing we can do.

The day of the ceremony
we take turns
taking showers,
brush our hair,
wear skirts and suits
just like we do each Christmas Eve.

But this time she will not greet us
with fragranced, soft skin,
sparkling costume jewelry,
and a hug that squeezes out
the sadness.

This is when we need that hug.

My brother will carry the coffin.
He worries that his shoes are scuffed,
his suit too tattered.
He tries to dye his shoes
in the last moments before the ceremony,
hoping they will dry in the sun.
But we all know
that she wouldn't mind what shoes he wore,
what suit he wore.
She only cared about the person within the shoes and suit.

In her last hours
in a morphine sleep
my brother whispered in her ear,
"I love you."
He was sure her rhythmic snoring paused.
He was sure she heard him,
his certainty easing pain.

Later that same day,
my aunt held the phone to my grandmother's ear
so I could say from far away,
"You are everything to me."
Through tears and breaking voice,
I tried to be as clear, as strong, as she.
But her snoring never broke an even tempo.
I don't think she heard me.
I think I called too late.

My father says repeatedly,
"She wanted it this way."
And this is true.
Every time I saw her, every Christmas, for years,
maybe for a decade,
she'd say,

"Don't you be sad for me when I'm gone.
I want you to know that I'm ready any time."
She'd been ready for years.
But I never was.

Glenelle recorded her story, her life
on a cassette tape years before she died.
She'd play it for us with pride in her eyes
as we gathered around the kitchen table.
We told her it was beautiful,
but we didn't want to think of it
didn't want to face the end.
But with all she created
in her very creative life,
this was her most inspired piece,
this was her life,
her words,
her masterpiece.

Sitting in the church that afternoon in mid-October
we hear that tape again.
The sun illuminates her face
still within the coffin,
her voice fills the sanctuary with softness,
a southern grace,
making it feel that she is with us.

I listen to her voice while looking at her,
so close to how it used to be,
but so so different.
I'm hungry for her words
in her own voice,
and cling to every detail
in ways I didn't when she was next to me.

An oral story full of love, friendship,

laughter, pain, and music unfolds.
Then in the church
with her so close,
her story ends.
Her voice is gone.
No more words, or music—
no Glenelle, no Grandmother.
No comfort.
Just silence.
Hollow
aching
silence.

The Threshold

BY PAUL BOARDMAN

> *"...beauty isn't all about just nice, loveliness like. Beauty is about more rounded substantial becoming. And I think when we cross a new threshold that if we cross worthily, what we do is we heal the patterns of repetition that were in us that had us caught somewhere. And in our crossing then we cross on to new ground where we just don't repeat what we've been through in the last place we were. So I think beauty in that sense is about an emerging fullness, a greater sense of grace and elegance, a deeper sense of depth, and also a kind of homecoming for the enriched memory of your unfolding life."*

—John O'Donohue[1]

It's early January, a busy season in death care. People hold on till after the holidays and then they let go. It's our second removal of the night. Irena died at age fifty-six. I wondered what would cause a woman my age to die. I feel so far from death but it happens. Indeed, death is happening all over. For every one million in population, as in greater Seattle, about thirty people die per day. Thirty people die per day in my city. Me and my removal crew, we take away about five or six of those thirty. Every day. We are harried, removing the dead. Who we remove includes those of every age, even fifty-six-year-olds. Irena. Her last name is Kozlow, which I assume is Polish.

When we arrive at the suburban house in Kirkland, Marcin, her husband, greets us at the door. He is about my age. And his son is there too. They are both pale and bald and have perfectly round European heads, like babes. They warmly invite us in and insist upon us, Wade and me, sitting down in their living room. Marcin speaks with a heavy accent but he is a man who is used to living in a foreign land: considering and mulling everything over before making any sudden move. He wants to ponder what

---

1 O'Donohue, John. "The Inner Landscape of Beauty." Interview. On Being (onbeing.org). February 28, 2008.

is next, along with us. He wants to ponder slowly, sitting down. He is inviting us to share with him the sequence. Now that his wife has died, he needs to know how to advance. He wants a choreographer to inform him of the steps we are going to take and the steps he is going to have to take next. He wants to get his footing, in this new life without his wife.

Marcin tells us, firmly but a little sheepishly, as though he wished he had more courage, that he doesn't want to witness his wife leaving their house; he doesn't want to see us carrying her out of his house, "For," he says softly, "that would be just too emotionally troubling." His son is in solidarity with him, nodding his head in agreement. The departure of their loved one, going out past their threshold, is upsetting. There is the inside space, their home, and there is the outside, all that exists out in the world; these are two very discrete spaces to them.

I am touched by the intensity and honesty of his acknowledgement that she is gone. There is something healthy about his psyche and his care. He is very deliberate. He believes in form. I assure him that we will be sensitive and that we will inform them when we are ready to take her into our care, out of their house. We will shield him from seeing her cross the threshold.

I ask him if he will take me upstairs to see his wife, in order to assess what equipment we will need to take her into our care. He complies. As he is leading me up the stairs, he tells me that she is "fresh" and that he has changed her into "new ready clothes." That sounds profound to me. I silently determine that I also want to be, in this life, in new, ready clothes.

In her room I see care. He has laid her out in state but has shrouded her carefully in a light bedspread. There are no wrinkles in the bedspread. He is a careful man. Across her tented face, running along the bridge of her European, leptorrhine nose, is a long-stemmed tulip, multi-colored. It is the most gentle preparation for a loved one's departure I have yet witnessed. Everything in the room, its tidiness, the muted tones, the good lighting, his orderliness, represents his care for her. I wonder, seeing this, if carefulness is one of our most important expressions of love. Carefulness conveys our tenderness. Carefulness is love in slowed-down time.

I review for him again what we are going to do: that we are going to get our backboard from the van and that when we come back we will wrap her up in a shroud, and that, when we are ready, we will go down to inform him that we are taking Irena out, so that he can retire to another room. He nods and says that when we inform him, he and his son will retreat to the other room downstairs, in the back past the kitchen. The plan is in place. He is feeling comfortable. "Yes, then we will hide," he declares. And then seemingly self-conscious about having used the word "hide," he wants affirmation and repeats, "But the English word 'hide' is the most appropriate in this situation, no?" And I assure him that it is. Absolutely. I am the grim reaper taking people's loved ones away from their homes, extracting them from the place of their belonging. Yes, it's something one might want to hide from.

We get the backboard from the van and come upstairs. Irena is light, she is a cancer featherweight. When I take off Marcin's attentively placed bedspread from her face, I see that he has tenderly tried to use a white elastic hairband, wrapped from crown to chin, to close her mouth, her slack jaw. Marcin is aesthetically sensitive to the gaping mouth of the dead. Anguished gape-mouth is bad. It is The Horror. The frozen Scream is bad. Open and closed is the difference between what is ghoulish and what is dignified. I so want all the mouths closed. I want this mouth closure so much that my developed expertise in Embalming Lab is the mandible suture—an invasive horrific mouth closure, where the sutures go through unimaginable places. It's a gruesome procedure that I do quite well. Because I want the mouth closed. Damn the Yawp. It's closure I want. Dignity is urgent and necessary. Marcin is my man.

We wrap Irena up and we strap her to the backboard. We tuck her soiled diaper in the plastic shroud with her, to be cremated. We lay our quilt over her. And put her on another bed to wait while we fold all the sheets carefully from her medical hospice bed and tidy up her aftermath to match Marcin's carefulness. I place the tulip back on the pillow of the now empty bed. Wade goes downstairs to alert Marcin and his son that we would be bringing Irena down and out through the front door. They retreat and hide. On our way out, we can hear them in the other room, their chatter deliberate white noise masking her Departure. We bring Irena out and lay her on a gurney and put her in the van, secure.

I head back to the house in order to say a proper goodbye to Marcin. The door is closed when I ring it, and I wonder if he doesn't want to see us anymore. But I wait. And he finally opens the door. I reach out to shake his hand but he refuses to take it. Instead, he steps over the threshold in a deliberate, exaggerated way in order to preserve the sacred space inside. Once he is on the landing OUTSIDE the house, he reaches to shake my hand vigorously and warmly.

"Thank you for your kindness and your understanding.... You are very professional but somehow..." He is raw and full of emotion. He is bowing his head like a Japanese person, and I bow back to him. I want to hug him and assure him but that would be inappropriate. There aren't any words. There are no assurances.

Dead

BY JENNIFER COATES

is dark
—black ice
that never melts.
You
do not stay
inside this word
but float to
me
in layered memories
that arrest
then slide
away
like years
fall
off a clock.

You come from
yesterday,
my childhood,
the uncertain space
carved between
mother and
grown-up
child.

I must find
another
word.

Countdown

BY PATRICIA A. NUGENT

In *Love, Medicine and Miracles,* Dr. Bernie Siegel cautions that no doctor should try to predict how long a terminal patient might live. There are too many variables; there are too many miracles. His practice as a surgeon has provided empirical evidence that healing stems from the mind and that unconditional love is the most powerful stimulant of the immune system.

My mother and I are both disciples of Dr. Siegel. We've read his books and can lend personal testimony to his message. Yet when my mother's doctor declares that a ten-day countdown has begun—that my mother will be dead in ten days—I simply choose to accept it.

I'm out of options.

"Miracles are still possible," my uncle reminds me. I wish I could believe that. My mother and I have been conjoined for nine months—as in the time preceding my birth. I've offered unconditional love and encouragement since she was diagnosed, yet she hasn't improved. And now I cannot wish her more time on this earth. Not even five minutes. Not like this.

I'm ready to say goodbye; it's time for her to go. There's little recognizable left of her spunk and beauty. All I can see is the disease.

That sounds cruel, I know. But I've been reduced to that, steeling myself against a cruel disease that demands a cruel prognosis. She's wanted to die for weeks, saying, "This isn't living, Patty. This is only existing."

Yet, now, I cannot discern if ten days is a long time or a short time. Will ten days seem forever as she continues to suffer emotionally and physically in this debilitated state? Or will ten days speed by, with me desperately clinging to delay a loss that will forever scar me?

Time takes on a whole new meaning. It's everything and nothing in the face of death. I know this now; it's not our first countdown.

– – –

"She may have had these tumors for years," the neurologist told us, so embedded are they in her brain. They could have been activated by stress, he supposed, the defective cells just waiting for the right biochemical mix to make their presence known—surreptitiously subdividing and multiplying.

Had I been aware of my mother's decline? I asked myself. Was it easier not to notice, to pretend that she was still invincible? I'd seen her stumble. Saw her drop her wallet, kick it, and still not realize she'd done so. I noticed her uncharacteristic forgetfulness but chalked it up to the strain of taking care of my father. After months of caregiving, she'd placed him in a nursing home, following a broken hip that compounded his dementia. But she was still at his side every day, advocating. Until she collapsed in her bathroom on an otherwise ordinary day, too embarrassed to use her emergency call button. A neighbor found her naked on the bathroom floor sometime later and placed a call from the Florida emergency room to my New York home.

I don't want to know how much time my mother spent alone, cold and wet on that ceramic tile, waiting for someone to find her. Or how much time had been wasted in getting her treatment. It doesn't matter now. Three brain tumors were detected, which seemed to have sprung up under her cranium overnight.

"Radiation won't save her but could buy her up to two years and alleviate the paralysis," the neurosurgeon told us. Or something like that. Who can remember?

I moved both parents back to New York State so I could watch over their care. We decided to keep my mother in the hospital during treatment, even though her doctors advised against it. "Hospitals are dirty places," one warned. "Take her home and bring her in for radiation every day." Although it seems counterintuitive, hospitals can jeopardize the recovery of people with weakened immune systems. But my mother insisted that she remain in the hospital so I wouldn't have to transport her daily to the medical facility forty-five minutes from my home. Besides, how would I have gotten her in and out of my car? She had already lost control over her left side.

Time stood still during my mother's hospital stay; days dragged on. Precious summer months that used to fly by lasted an eternity; July and August were spent anxiously waiting for a reprieve from the disease. It was the slowest summer, the longest summer, the worst summer.

Seven long weeks spent waiting for that miracle.

Big black X's marked off each day on a large calendar that she could see from her bed. Each X brought us closer to the end of treatment. Thirty-four X's in all, as we waited for an indication that what she went through was worth it. A simple twitch of a toe on her left foot would have satisfied us, so desperate were we.

Time morphed into a demonic, unassailable creature. It even paralyzed this high-strung daughter when I realized that all my prior planning, time management, and imposed efficiencies became irrelevant. There was nothing for me to do but wait for it to claim my mother.

"You've been a real trouper," the staff told her as she left the hospital in an ambulance headed to a long-term care facility. As a souvenir, they ceremoniously handed her the mask that she had to wear during radiation treatments—like Darth Vader's.

When faced with our family's collective despondency about the lack of results, the radiologist offered another countdown: "There still could be some positive effects from all that radiation floating around in her body. There's a chance it just hasn't kicked in yet; we need to wait a little longer. Give it another six weeks."

Paradoxically, the crisp fall days flew by as we raced to the end of the period during which we could possibly have noted some benefit from the radiation. Not unlike the ride home seeming shorter than the ride out. Every day we searched for signs that she was improving. We hoped for more lucidity, more movement, something to show she was returning to her old self. Nothing. Thirty-four treatments with nothing to show for them. Except a bald head, undeniable despair, and the mask she used as a storytelling prop to relay her treatment trauma to visitors. Until my sister threw it away, insisting, "We don't need such a perverse reminder of that time."

As "Jingle Bells" began to fill the air, my mother admitted she knew she was dying. Our collective false bravado no longer worked. She lost her will to live; she begged God to let her die. I too sent intercessions to the heavens on her behalf, although selfishly I wanted to hold on to her forever.

– – –

Now another doctor starts us on a new countdown: ten days. Ten more dinners, ten more visits, ten more, ten more, ten more. Or maybe only three. Or one. "Things can happen very quickly at this stage," the nurse warns. "We may not even have time to call you." So I must wait here—be here—with my mother as she waits to die.

In retrospect, it's hard to justify how we collectively spent her last few months. The radiation didn't buy her any time; we're far short of the two years we'd bargained for. Should we have done something more—taken her to the Mayo Clinic? Or done less— taken her home? I'm trying to quell my regrets because I'll never know.

After death, time will be rendered powerless. Right now, I am.

But in our remaining time together—whether five minutes, five weeks, or five months—I know what I will do: I will hold her. Whisper my devotion in her ear. Hold her hand. Stroke her head. Reassure her. Outline the contour of her face with my fingers so I can commit my mother's face to memory. That's all I'll have left— memory. It may seem macabre, but I wish I had her radiation mask. It was form-fitted to her face, outlining her fine features. Like the Shroud of Turin.

I bring my father to say goodbye to his wife of sixty-three years. He doesn't recognize her at first, a consequence of his dementia and her disease. "I'll be back next week," he promises in an uncharacteristic lucid moment. "Will you still be here?"

She tightens her grip on his arm but doesn't answer his question. She stares into his face as if trying to memorize it, to take it with her. As I am doing with her face.

Her doctor had given her ten days.

She's proving him wrong.

No doctor should try to predict how long a terminal patient might live.

Silent Messages Heard

BY SALLY SHOWALTER

"I feel like I'm eighteen again and something bad is going to happen," my brother Terry told me. A few days earlier my father began vomiting uncontrollably. The doctor's tests revealed it was due to a massive heart attack. My father survived a quadruple bypass sixteen years prior, and an aneurism surgery behind his stomach wall. He had been on dialysis for four years due to kidney damage. These collective conditions did not add up in his favor.

Terry had been with our dad since the night he was flown to St. John's Hospital. He had seen the ventilator that covered Dad's thin face; seen the long pipe that was jammed down his throat that disappeared at the parting of his lips; and had seen various tubes braided loose to and from the seven machines on small wheels with buttons, switches, and lights blinking in different colors. He had seen Dad try to speak when he opened his eyes, struggle against the straps that carefully tied him to the side of the bed, and seen the bag hanging out below the sheet. For four days he had seen Dad close his eyes too many times. I was about to.

Terry led the way along the polished floors and tinted white walls of the hospital. I followed his oversized, big brother body and gray hair that grew long enough to cover the back of his neck. He opened the door to reveal Dad's head tilted to his right side, with machines of blue plastic and clear plastic, containing oxygen all around him. My heart did a slam dunk right in the middle of my chest.

I held Dad's arm, my fingers turning numb from the icebox conditions of the room. The doctor and his team arrived, telling us what we didn't want to hear. Without the forest of machines and tubes, Dad would have a flat field with no growth. There was no hesitation on our part to yield to my father's wishes—yet none of us could actually say the clump of words, so instead stood together in silent agreement.

The ventilator caused him to struggle; his head rocked

back and forth while he tried to speak. His throat was raw and inflamed and his eyelids fluttered like a newborn wet butterfly. I spoke to him by repeating a mantra of family names he loved: Hettie, Terry, Mom, Tene, Lennie, and others. Dad shook his head up and down.

"Do you understand me? Can you hear me?"

He tried so very hard to speak.

"Dad, maybe you can't say what you want, but God can hear your thoughts and he will remember."

Later, as the afternoon began to lengthen and tire, a button was snapped off, a line removed, and a machine wheeled away. Little by little, my father's lifelines were taken away. We were asked to leave while they removed the ventilator. Once we returned, Dad looked younger and rested, with a small oxygen line to his nose.

My brother kept a physical distance from our dad's bed. He sat in our mom's wheelchair and spun in slow-motion circles while she sat in a hospital recliner, wrapped in her coat, a blanket cocooned around her. Our family friend Susan got up for a smoke and I wagged my finger at her. She wore a red T-shirt for Dad that read St. Louis Cardinals, since he was a big fan of the team. Was? He is…*is* a Cardinals fan.

I asked Susan to drive Mom home. Her exhaustion came out in short and raspy breaths. My niece arrived with fleece pullovers for me and two of our cousins. The five of us sat or stood in Dad's room, catching up with quiet laughs and silent looks. Eventually, everyone left through the big doors while I sat alone with Dad and smoothed his hair.

I played a few of his favorite melodies from my iPhone and held it close to his ear. With my hand on his arm, the other on his knee, I spoke of when he farmed, vacations to Colorado, his love for fishing and reading, a favorite book. He moved his head up and down like a yes, his chin resting again on his chest, my hand warm on his cool palm. He suddenly rolled his eyelids halfway up and I lowered my face down to make eye contact. He looked directly at me, and, behind the veil of cloudy white, I saw the blue in his eyes, the hint of green, a second, and I was the one not breathing. He closed his eyes—two breaths, a soft puff-puff under his gown—and then nothing.

I dashed out of the room to the nurses' station. "I think you should look at my dad."

All six eyes went straight to the monitors, and they quickly snapped out of their chairs. The nurses checked the pulse at Dad's ankles, listened with their stethoscopes, and soon gave their condolences. I believed each one to be sincere; it was in their eyes, their long hours of night shifts, and their reason for choosing this career.

They touched my arm as they left the room so I could be alone with my father. I looked at my father, just three weeks past his ninetieth birthday, so frail and vulnerable, no longer able to protect himself. I heard his place of being my father depart. I heard the silence. I heard the words still wedged in his heart.

When It's Time

BY LEE KAREN STOW

I sense they come for you
Opening arms wide and
lifting you from my side
Stretching our cord
Snapping us apart

Three days and two nights
Quietly in this room with
'Welcome Maureen'
written above your bed
Side by side
Fading from me

Your skin smooth as porcelain
Arms tucked beneath a blanket
Your red hair washed
pretty in nightie stripes
Your mouth open,
turns to hear when I remind you,
I'm here, Mam
beside you.

Friends come to say goodbye
Lay blue Rosary beads on your pillow.
We talk, distracted.
Silence. Stillness.
Skin so white, breath no more
Sneaking away from me.
I howl, like a baby pulling in pain
Letting you go
Letting me go.

I sense they have come for you
See you rise
floating to them. Joy! Joy!
Your being fills the room with calm
softness, lightness
the fullness of pure love.
I open the door to let you fly
Away from your name above the bed

You brought me life
I help you to die.
So when will you come for me?
I know, I know, not just yet
You want me to see, to heal.
But when you do come for me
To lift me to your side
I'll be ready, Mam.

Life After Life

The Presence of her absence is

everywhere.

—Edna St. Vincent Millay

the day after i killed myself

BY NYANISO TUTU-BURRIS

the day after i killed myself, my mum came into my room at
    6:12 a.m. to wake me up
she sang to me "rise and shine"
but my soul had already risen—and i was no longer shining
i watched her sit on my bed
and brush my hair out of my face
i fell in love with the way she rubbed my back
and kissed my cheek
i fell in love with the way the sun shone off the dew drops of
    tears that sprinkled her face
i fell in love with my nine-year-old sister who was not mad
nor confused
she knew what death was as it had haunted my house many
    times
but the last whisper of a childhood had escaped her lips the
    second i breathed my last breath.

the day after i killed myself, i walked to my grandparents'
    house
i saw my grandfather having Eucharist
and catching his breath when he said my name in prayers
i saw my grandmother shaking with tears
because she would have to bury her own granddaughter
long before herself
i saw them say the Lord's Prayer, with confusion in their
    eyes
wondering why God would let me go.

the morning after i killed myself, i watched the news
i saw the photographers swarming outside my house
not giving my family a moment to grieve

my sister was bombarded
my mother was hassled
i was gone.

the morning after i killed myself, i ran to the hospital
i pleaded with the doctors
screamed at my lifeless body
begging her to please wake up
but it was too late.

Worrying the Beads toward Something like Grace

BY STEPHEN MEAD

Years before you passed, Mom, I recall reading that many religions say a certain number of prayers for the dead, based on the number of years the deceased had been alive. I meditated on this as I walked through the backyard of the farm where we shared years of our lives. It was one of those fusty humid days where heat shimmers and the variety of insects busily buzzing created a sort of Zen reverie. As a person born with an innate creative nature, I have often found myself in these dreamy states, not preoccupied (since I am aware of the present) so much as cognizant that another part of myself is deeply focused on a theme, an image that develops into others like an internal phrase or word becoming the building blocks of a poem.

Over the years I organically adopted this practice as a way of praying for those I have loved and lost. This is a chant of sorts, sung in an almost-whisper inside my head. If my husband has left for work, I get brave and sing them out loud. These prayers do not come from any pages of organized religion. Though they have the O.C.D. repetitiveness of rosary beads or worry beads, they are a bit more free-form. They are a one-sided conversation I don't expect anyone to answer. The prayers are sacred: kind of a secret for the person I'm praying to. My conversations create a spiritual home for that person inside of me, adding depth to the dimension of closeness, which must have already been there somehow. I always begin my prayer to you with, "I can still see your face, Mom."

A part of these daily prayers is rooted, selfishly, almost unconsciously, in anxiety/depression (for as you used to say to yourself and passed on to me, "Don't let your nerves get the best of you"). I chant, "I pray you are enjoying your afterlife, Mom, in absolute bliss, happiness, lightness, energy, and love. No more worries. No more fears. No more pain." Yes, I suppose that is rather sentimentally New Age-like and vague, but I think it gives enough outline for not only my mom, but for others who have passed (and even for a greater deity) to add their own palette of colors. I imagine those colors taking shape in water on a white background, perhaps that (more MGM sentimental stuff here) of a cloud. I can also imagine these colors taking shape in water that already has a spectrum of hues, and that the spirit adds its own natural shades of radiance to the mix.

Over the years, I've become someone who doesn't particularly take comfort in the idea that our loved ones' spirits hover about us, chained to us as unseen watchers from the sky. Considering daily digestion and necessary bowel functions, the idea of having a benevolent voyeur watching all this is pretty disconcerting. I much prefer the idea that the loved one has gone on, as if visiting another country on a majestic unseen plane and is having new good experiences.

I imagine your afterlife, as well as parts of your life when I didn't know you. While praying, visuals unfold in my mind, and the textures are sometimes so rich I can almost touch them. I see your high school graduation and your marriage to Dad as a slideshow in my head, a film strip forming, dissolving, reforming. And by doing so, I feel as if I experienced the events a little by loving you through them, knowing what milestones they were for you, and, ultimately, our family history.

I certainly hope this does not tie you to the earth. It seems to me the sum total of life could actually be considered the weight of human experience, the gravity that holds any one of us to this plane. After passing, it would be great if our soul could experience lightness and feel a sort of loving forgiveness, even folly. If the mortal experience has had its share of trauma, then perhaps when looking back on it, the spirit deserves a passage of separate peace, a place of ultimate grace, the healing borne of an understanding that is necessary in order to move on. What this separate peace will require, without emotional freight, is simply empathy and an omniscient perspective of the whole picture and whatever factored into it. Then peace and reconciliation can occur by letting go.

Saying prayers to you, Mom, I suppose is an attempt to believe that our death can be a peaceful transition to our next phase. I don't have a definitive answer to what happens when we die, but

I like to think we live on in some way, perhaps through the loved ones we left behind. If this is true, I know you are alive in me.

"I can still see your face, Mom."

Hello from Heaven!

BY SHERRY RIND

First the streamers
shoot iridescent pink and green
curls against the night sky
and fireworks foam noiselessly
like falling stars.
I hear ballroom music, tinny
with distance, and the cruiser
appears southeast of Venus,
its tiny figures waving hello,
the weather's fine, don't worry
about us. We're having the time
of our lives.

Usually I'm elbow deep in dinner's debris
or shoving my son's nose at his homework.
Why can't they call when I'm dressed
and ready to go?
Not that they'd notice
corporeal detail. I don't worry
about them but what they left—
the crockery and dressers, paintings
and promises, all flotsam
to which the living cling
to keep afloat.

So I yell toward heaven
where they're having a ball,
what can I hope for? They wave
and laugh, even the shy grandmother
got up in a beaded blue dress,

rhinestones in her silver hair,
kicking up a glass slipper.

See you later
is all they ever say.

A Love Story

BY ANN MAYO

Knowing angels are real is easy; sensing that we have loving spirits surrounding us is wonderful; believing people have twin flames is somewhat plausible; having it all happen at once caused me to know there are no accidents. Everything happens for a reason.

The story begins on a hot August day as I was coming home from work, totally exhausted, not at all clean and not at all happy. I was even less happy when I got a flat tire and realized my cell was dead and I couldn't call any of my sons to help me install the spare. Grudgingly, I got out of the car and prepared to change the flat. Within a few minutes an 'old guy' in a gray truck pulled up behind my car and walked toward me. Really, he was just a few years older than I.

And so began a love story. As he spoke, I felt myself surrounded by a rectangular, pulsating blue bubble filled with thousands of shining, tiny blue bubbles. He asked if I needed help, and although my first thought was to say something like, "Do you really think I enjoy being on my knees in gravel?" I held my tongue and said, "Yes." He gently pushed me aside and as he worked we spoke. He was also divorced, and, being a teacher, he was off for the summer. He said he would get the tire repaired and I could pick it up at his home the next day, but only if he could make dinner for me. It was out of character for me to accept his offer, but, whatever had happened in the brief time we spoke, I knew I was safe with him. Maybe it was his strong arms on my shoulders as I was about to leave.

The next day arrived, and, without any sense of what was to come, I arrived at his home and was treated to a wonderful barbequed salmon dinner. He took me on a tour of his home, and then we sat outside to watch the sunset and filled the hours with much talk and laughter of days gone by, going back to school in our older years, and his promises of taking me on a fishing trip, but mostly there was an overriding sense that we had truly connected at the soul level. I felt "at home."

When I said I had to leave, he looked surprised.

"Aren't you staying the night?" he asked.

"I wasn't invited."

"You will never need an invitation."

Two days later we were living together.

It became a time of incredible peace. I felt I was finally where I had always wanted to be. Our days were filled with fishing and camping; entertaining; enjoying our children, colleagues, family, and friends; and always those hours of just talking. We went to rugby games and drank beer and laughed until it hurt. He continually surprised me with gifts of wildflowers and beautiful cards. We planned a future of growing old together.

Then the lump appeared on his head, and it was followed by years of undiagnosed cancer. When it was finally diagnosed, there were months wasted on a treatment plan. We shared the news with friends and family, and I accompanied him to every appointment. Valuable time had been wasted by the misdiagnosis, and the cancer spread to his lungs and spine. It was a time of unbearable pain, but holding on to each other lessened it for him.

After each treatment, we spoke of the fishing trips we would take and our winter home in Costa Rica. We both knew that would never happen, but to speak otherwise would have been too hurtful. We had an unspoken agreement that we would never talk of death.

Then came the news from the cancer clinic: there were no more treatments, and the only thing we could do was decide if he would die at home or in the hospital. We refused to listen to the doctor and I took him home, where we were sure he would get better.

The last days came all too soon, and I had to bring him back to the hospital. Three years, four months, and sixteen days of loving, joy, secrets, laughter, and living life to the fullest ended. I was alone in the hospital room with him when he took his last breath. I watched his soul rise, gave him a soft kiss on the cheek, and said, "I'll see you soon."

Maybe there could have been more for us to say, but those words might have also foretold of death, a reality neither of us believed in. I think we both said all that was in our hearts through our silent conversations of looking into each other's eyes and smiling.

Although his soul departed, he didn't leave me. One day when I was driving way too fast, a firm hand slapped me on the arm. There was no one in the car with me. Another time I was walking along a forest trail with a girlfriend and talking about Lew. She stopped me and pointed down to the ground, where there was a cluster of heart-shaped rocks. "Lew is still watching over you, you know," she said.

I still have the remnants of the first bouquet he gave me, and even now as I hold the twigs, I feel him around me, simply smiling and remembering. Although it has been thirteen years, a friend's words back then prove to be true. "The time between now and until you're together again will be less than one of God's heartbeats."

Blue

BY RAJ PERSAUD

At sixty-seven years, my companion, Blue, was at the stage in his life when he was getting ready to reap the benefits of the life as he had envisioned it should be—one of leisure and total freedom to pursue his own interests. But when a persistent backache could not be healed through massage, physical therapy, or pain relievers, he conceded to further testing. The results revealed he had stage four multiple myeloma (cancerous plasma cells).

Outwardly, Blue showed no change in attitude even after learning the news. He had a zest for life and an optimism while maintaining a stoicism that was at once inspiring yet surprising. These qualities, which accompanied him at all times, were largely a product of surmounting many difficulties in his life, both personal and medical.

The life of a cancer patient can be calibrated against the physical, mental, and emotional drama that is played out each minute. If it can be said that no two minutes of our normal daily life are exactly the same, this is so much more true of the patient of cancer. Each minute, the drama unfolded and the colors changed, ranging the gamut of human emotions: from hues of rose-colored rays of hope to the black clouds of dejection and anguish. At times, the pain became unbearable and the thick clouds of confusion engulfed him.

Friends and associates encouraged me, "Now is the time to do whatever you two wanted." I chose not to heed the dire warnings of those who had been through similar experiences with their loved ones. I reasoned, medicine had evolved quite recently in the most dramatic ways, with the headline-grabbing breakthroughs in immunotherapy. While this idea was still in its infancy, recent examples of the use of this technology, including the story of former President Jimmy Carter's fight with stage four cancer, demonstrated the huge successes in the treatment of cancer. According to the Cancer Research Society, the survival rate for Canadians diagnosed with cancer rose from forty percent in 1975 to over sixty percent thirty years later in 2015, and from fifty-six to sixty-three percent over the last decade.

In spite of these statistics, which were encouraging, the largest factor that colored my evaluation of Blue's chances was what I was seeing—a man, physically, mentally, and spiritually resolute to the onslaught of the disease. Through all of the physical, emotional, and spiritual challenges, Blue never let go of an inherent faith in the hospital and doctors. Blue was a diabetic, and, during the last five years of his life, he had undergone a triple bypass, as well as having a stent placed in an artery. He came through these procedures with flying colors and was extremely grateful for the exceptional medical attention he received during these operations. The experiences had primed him for similar successes in his current medical treatment. He had an unshakeable belief that his doctors would eventually find a solution to get him back on his feet. After all, what disease or surgery could be as bad as that of heart disease?

He also maintained a positive outlook on all experiences or incidents. One day, he had an accident and spilled food all over the floor. The attendant nurse was harsh and was heard yelling at him with a loud voice. On listening to the yelling, his neighbor in the room, an old lady in her nineties, started crying in sympathy with Blue. A day later, when Blue and I were discussing the incident, I asked how he was feeling about it. He responded, "Yesterday and its problems and challenges are gone. Let's face today with a new set of eyes."

He was put through a radiation treatment as a temporary solution for the pain. After radiation, his medical team would determine the treatment plan that would attack the actual cancer cells. With radiation, Blue's pains started to ease. Once again, hope and faith raised their brightly hued colors and the clouds lifted.

Through the fog, Blue seemed to emerge with a renewed sense of self. For the first time since his diagnosis, he seemed ready to make contact with the outside world by calling a friend. He was already thinking of making plans to return home and wanted his friend to work on a home renovation project in preparation for the move.

Before he could solidify his plans with his friend, the pain returned and, with it, new medical concerns. All around the hospital floor, similar drama was being played out. And as each progressed to its own finale, it brought home more than ever the notion that Blue could be the next in line to be called. The looks on the faces of those who understood only too well the import of the diagnosis was something I'll never forget. On one of the first nights, when I was still wondering how bad Blue's condition rated, the attendant said, "This is so hard on the family." It wasn't the words but rather the look she gave us that spoke volumes. Blue saw that look, but, to my relief, it did nothing to curb his tenacity and positive outlook.

One evening Blue was lying down, and I was sitting as usual, at the foot of his bed. We were watching television—the stock market—and discussing stocks. To a casual observer, it was a normal evening, under normal circumstances. A patient on the same floor, a kindly lady, peered her head around the curtained wall and came into the room for a chat and quick visit. She was a long-term outpatient at the hospital and wondered the usual question: "What did the doctor say today?" Blue and I looked at each other, a look that said so many different things. What to tell her? It seemed such an innocuous question. Blue read the tone and meaning behind the question, and he saw it in her eyes: a mixture of empathy, friendliness, maybe some pity—all in one. Blue's response, "Nothing new," left so much unsaid, although his heart was full. On to small talk, then she left.

With each passing day, more intense doses of pain medication were required and with it an intense fear belied my outward appearance. A fear of what, I wasn't sure, but it grew daily.

Many questions and fears arose while witnessing his pain and experiencing my own. Blue was not ready to go, and we were not ready to let him go yet. His passing would leave a vacuum in my life. How would I fill this void? I needed to find answers to all the questions and the reasons to explain the purpose of suffering. It didn't make sense that each of us spends inordinate, if not all, portions of our lives on birth, work, enjoyment of life, then, as often as not, we are gone without any time to prepare.

Going about our daily routine, we seldom expect a sudden calamity, sudden bad news, or tragedy. When it happens, it is a stark reminder that we have no control of our timetable, which has already been set. The suddenness catches us unprepared. Toward the last days, I saw how Blue was in a hurry to get his worldly affairs in order. But who could tell what his innermost thoughts were? What home did he envision going to? What more did he hope to do, and, what, if any, changes would he make, given the time? I could only guess, from the sadness in his eyes while in the firm grip of the disease.

One day his breathing labored. Into the night it continued. He uttered the only words in the next twelve-hour period, "I am going home."

Blue passed away the next morning, Sunday, July 12, 2015. He had been diagnosed with stage four cancer on May 5th, two months earlier. He had thrived on hope, and to admit defeat, even for one second, would be to admit that the gift of life was being withdrawn, and that would be death, even before it occurred. He went the way he wanted to, with all his hopes of a miracle intact until these last moments. I held his hand to the end, no words of goodbye, only a comforting nearness, and then it was over. But is it ever over for the one who has gone on, or the one who is left to continue on?

Growing up in an orthodox Hindu home, I was taught from the earliest stage I can remember that God is a fair and loving God. I had always believed and took this belief at face value. I didn't have a serious desire to seek out the deeper mystery. My life was proceeding smoothly enough, and I felt that I had total control of my life and my destiny.

My father, a Hindu priest, had worked tirelessly to get his children to learn and practice the teachings of our scriptures, including regular prayers and meditation. We were good students for the most part, although occasionally falling short of his expectations. After his passing a few years ago, I became more eager to learn all I could of the core spiritual and philosophical concepts in Hindu mythology. The literature is vast, and, as I read, I was gaining more insight into what my father had tried so hard to pass on to us while he was alive.

At Blue's passing, I once again turned to my own Hindu faith, looking for answers. I sought out select texts and listened to lectures and presentations of scholarly saints on the subject of the purpose of life. The Bhagavad Gita, or Gita as it is known, is one of the most well-known of Hindu texts. Mahatma Gandhi referred to the Gita as his "spiritual dictionary." Estimated to date back to fifth to second century BC, the Gita contains the essence of the Vedas—Sanskrit texts said to be the oldest books of mankind at 5000 years BC and believed to have been revealed to ancient saints and transmitted orally.

I had read the Gita many times, but now I studied it from a changed, more purposeful perspective. According to the Gita, the soul is never born, so it never dies—it is immortal. At the time of death, when the body dies, the soul, based on karma—what you sow, you shall reap—migrates into another body. The cycle of birth and death of the body continues until a state of "purity" is achieved through practice of great karma. At that time, one becomes "self-realized." This occurs when the little, or individual, Self, or soul, merges with the Divine. Buddha is an example of a great soul who achieved such self-realization.

The Gita states that we mortals, since we have been given the gift of the human body, have an opportunity, through the practice of meditation, to experience moments of the same bliss that the great souls experience. It explains that, during these moments, the insights into cosmic truths would guide one to performing right actions; right actions in turn produce good karma, ultimately resulting in a self-realized soul and ending the cycle of birth and death.

With Blue's passing, and having already been exposed from an early age to some of the merits of meditation, I embarked on a schedule of daily routine practice. At first, I found many aspects of the practice too demanding, requiring a discipline and mental concentration that did not come naturally. As soon as I sat down to start, the uninvited thoughts would come rushing in, as if deliberately setting out to usurp my intention. Through maintaining a constant and regular routine, the process became easier, and, with each successful effort, more fulfilling.

As I have also continued with the readings on Hindu philosophy, I recently came upon a treatise called the Kaivalya Upanishad. The Upanishads are a body of work written around the period between 800 BC and 500 BC. They include approximately two hundred texts, which elaborate on the highest philosophical concepts of the Vedas. The Kaivalya Upanishad has provided me with some clear insights into the process for acquiring the state of mental peace that one aims for in meditation.

It describes that knowledge of the Self is secret—secret, because it is hidden behind the many layers of our personality. It states that to understand this Self when in meditation, one's thoughts must move across the layers: starting from the gross, to the most subtle, gross being defined as the physical body; going beyond layer of mind and senses to the next subtler layer, that of ego and intellect; and after this layer of ignorance (of God's laws), beyond even the layer of bliss.

This visualization provided by the Kaivalya Upanishad is a concept that has helped me identify and understand the nature of the thoughts, which try to invade the mind to let it wander aimlessly. With this knowledge, I can more easily ward off the unwelcome thoughts. As I continue to practice applying the insights I have acquired, there are moments during meditation when I experience true peace. In these moments, all things seem possible. All fears dissolve, all prayers are answered—prayers of peace, contentment, and a reasoning born of intuition. It puts physical suffering in perspective.

In the stillness of those moments, I can sense Blue's spirit. Based on the law of karma, I don't know if, when, and where he has acquired another physical body, but I know that the soul exists. It feels no pain, no suffering.

To his dying breath, Blue did not utter the word "cancer." He never gave a name to the disease, no acknowledgement of the enemy. As if by doing so, it could not harm him. And our religion teaches that this is true: no harm can ever come to the soul, as we are *sat chit Ananda*—pure being, consciousness, and bliss eternal.

One does not have to wait for tragedy, or death; neither does one have to be a recluse to experience the joy of meditation. The Gita describes that meditation and the ensuing intuition do not preclude us from carrying out our mundane responsibilities; rather, the refined clarity of vision that comes from this intuition should guide us toward increased awareness, focus, and creativity in performing our worldly duties to the best of our ability. In doing so, we would be fulfilling our purpose on earth.

I feel that, even though the pain lingers, in a true sense, there is no loss. Each event, including death, represents a step in a cycle toward another pre-set destination. Through this understanding, I am emerging stronger and trying to determine more ways to better fulfill my own purpose on earth.

Before now, I have been looking for answers from the outside world. The answers I was seeking—by divine Grace—were already within me. I only needed the key to finding them.

Morning

BY DONNA HILBERT

You come to me in a dream
dressing for your pre-dawn ride,
just as you did on the morning
that you died, awakening me
when you turn on the light
to find some missing socks.
I scolded you then,
but now I plead, appeal to reason:
since you know
what's going to happen
please don't go.
You touch my hair, pull on your jersey,
ride again into that dark morning.

Author Bios

As a child, Andrea Adams drew from her books and imagination by making paper dolls. These early "characters" started her on the path to a lifetime of storytelling. She kept journals and wrote letters about her adventures as a young adult engaged in careers in alternative energy, human resources, marketing, environmental nonprofit management and ecotourism. Her recent writings include "Bernese Buddha" in *Secret Histories: Stories of Courage, Risk, and Revelation,* edited by Brenda Peterson, and "Lake MacDonald" for *The Inside Trail,* edited by John Hagen. She is currently working on a book about an unusual parenting odyssey.

Beth Rahe Balas is an artist, art teacher, and garden designer who impulsively fled to the Pacific Northwest almost 30 years ago after nearly dying from anaphylactic shock. There she found sea air, moss, and ferns on an island near Seattle where she still lives with her husband, two grown children, dogs, and chickens. Her poem remembers an intense and strange time in college when death took many friends and lovers.

Kim Beyer is the author of fourteen science fiction, poetry, and comparative religion books. She is a yoga therapist and qigong teacher, as well as an adult education professional, working and playing in northern Michigan. Please visit her blog at: www. guhacaveoftheheart.blogspot.com.

Suzy Blough has been actively involved in the field of International Education for more than twenty years, and has studied, lived, worked, and traveled throughout the world. Currently Suzy holds the position of Program Coordinator with the Georgia Council for International Visitors (GCIV), creating valuable experiences for emerging leaders from around the world and opportunities for Georgians to be globally engaged. Suzy received her B.A. from Emory University and her M.Ed. from UGA. She has been happily married to Doug Blough, a professor at GA Tech, for twenty-four years; has two daughters in college; and has Goldie, a loveable, lazy mutt!

Paul Boardman is a writer and Funeral Celebrant living in Seattle, Washington. He grew up in Tokyo, Japan, and holds the farcically-named "Masters of Divinity" from Princeton. Two of his enduring thematic obsessions in writing are: what constitutes a good life in the face of death/loss and the nature of yearning, even greed, for love.

Dr. Karen Breeck is a retired Canadian military flight surgeon. She has worked and traveled to over sixty countries and looks forward to someday reaching that magic 100 number. She is presently divorced and is a Calgary, Alberta, transplant now living in Ottawa, Ontario, Canada.

Chanel Brown holds a master's degree in English from Western Washington University, where she studied creative nonfiction and served as the nonfiction editor for the *Bellingham Review*. She was born and raised in Yakima, Washington, and now lives in Seattle.

Nyaniso Tutu-Burris is a feminist, emerging activist, and a first year Theology student. She is the eldest daughter of Mpho Tutu and the fifth grandchild of Archbishop Emeritus Desmond Tutu. In 2011, Nyaniso moved with her mother and sister to Cape Town, South Africa, where she recently graduated from St. Cyprian's all girls' school. She is now studying at the University of the Western Cape in Cape Town. Like her grandfather, Nyaniso stands up for what she believes in. In recent keynote addresses from South Africa to Sweden to the U.S. she inspired young people to get out in the world and make a difference.

When Dane Chapin's father passed away in 2013 he came upon the idea of creating a book of tributes to those we have lost, drawing together a community of people from around the world. From that idea comes this book, *Just A Little More Time*. Dane enjoys writing poetry for his wife, Katherine, and political commentary and satire. He is a serial entrepreneur and serves as chairman of two companies he founded: Zephyr Partners, a San Diego-based real estate development company, and USAOPOLY, a maker of toys and games. In his spare time, he plays golf, skis, and spends time with his children. He is a San Diego native and is fortunate to split time between there and Aspen, Colorado.

Jennifer ("Jenny") Coates moved to Bainbridge Island, WA, with her husband, Samuel Brody, a classical pianist, and her now sixteen-year-old daughter, Cymbeline Brody, in 2006. She is an international tax, transactional tax, and business lawyer by trade, but has many other interests which fill her days, including writing poetry. Jenny's poems have been published in several anthologies, in *Ars Poetica*, and as part of the Bainbridge Island Poetry Corners celebration of National Poetry Month. Jenny frequently shares these poems, which helped her navigate her own grief, with friends who have lost people important to them, in hopes others will find them of comfort as well.

Wendy Staley Colbert's personal essays have been featured in *The Huffington Post, Salon, Jezebel, Whole Life Times, ParentMap, This Great Society, Writing in Public, Feel More Better, and Writing Is My Drink*, and in the anthologies *We Came to Say* and *We Came Back to Say*. Her essays are also featured in Kerry Cohen's anthology, *Spent*, from Seal Press, and in the anthology *Three Minus One*, from She Writes Press. She was an inaugural cast member of *Listen To Your Mother—Seattle* in 2015. Wendy holds an MFA from Pacific University and is working on a memoir. www.wendystaleycolbert.com.

Elizabeth Coplan, Playwright and Founder of *The Grief Dialogues*, is a forty+-year PR and marketing veteran. Her professional and life experiences in numerous cities throughout the U.S., including New York City, San Antonio, Los Angeles, and Seattle, create an unending library of writing themes. Her award-winning play, *Hospice: A Love Story*, was performed on Bainbridge Island, WA; Seattle, WA; Sedona, AZ; and ran for six weeks at The Group Rep in Los Angeles at the Lonny Chapman Theatre.

Debra D'Angelo is a sacred ecofeminist living in the Pacific Northwest on an island surrounded by the Salish Sea. She states, "I often become part of a dreamlike story where every tree is sacred and the planet responds as a living and breathing friend guiding me through symbols, synchronicity, the birds and animals...even the clouds will offer me support and direction...I spend a great deal of time in prayer in the wild."

Lori Davila is an author and career, resume, and interviewing expert. She has coached thousands of professionals and executives around the world at companies that include Delta Air Lines, The Coca Cola Company, General Electric, and IBM. Lori has contributed to *The Wall Street Journal*, *The Washington Post*, *Los Angeles Times*, and *Business Management Asia*. Her book titles include *How to Choose the Right Person for the Right Job Every Time* (McGraw-Hill) and *Perfect Phrases for Perfect Hiring* (McGraw-Hill), and she is also a contributing author of the book *Conscious Women - Conscious Careers*. In the last few years Lori helped several close family members transition to the place beyond this earthly life.

Sheryl Burpee Dluginski holds an MA in Journalism and a Certificate in Science Reporting from New York University. She attended the Yale Writers Conference last summer and was a writing resident at Renaissance House in the Catskills this summer. The granddaughter of Dr. Royal H. Burpee, creator of the popular high-intensity functional training movement, the Burpee, Sheryl is owner and founder of Generations Fitness, LLC, a private health and fitness training company. She is the author of the as yet unpublished memoir, *Wasteland Reclaimed: Finding Love in the Wake of Incest*. More information about her work and writing is at www.sherylburpeedluginski.com.

Kathleen LaFrancis Eaton, Ph.D., was born into a military family in Texas and grew up moving every few years. She is a novelist working on the second in a series of thrillers. Her gardening column and essays can be accessed via her website. Inspiration for memoir poetry was a direct result of writing this piece, which brought back the richness of a gift that has lasted a lifetime. Kathleen lives in a small town north of Seattle with her husband. KathleenEaton.net

James Anthony Ellis is an award-winning playwright, journalist, and filmmaker, who is the author of six books, including the *The Honor Book*. James's next book, *Huh? The Joys, Sorrows, and Comic Relief of Miscommunication*, will be released in 2016. Connect at LegacyProductions.org and JimEllis1103@yahoo.com.

Barbara Eknoian's work has appeared in *Pearl, Chiron Review, Cadence Collective Anthology, YDP,* and Silver Birch Press's *Green, Summer,* and *Self-Portrait* poetry anthologies. She has been twice-nominated for a Pushcart Prize and is an ongoing member of Donna Hilbert's poetry workshop. Her latest novel, *Monday's Child,* and her poetry book, *Why I Miss New Jersey,* are available at Amazon. She lives in La Mirada with her extended family, son, daughter, and three grandsons.

Marianne Goldsmith is the pen-name of Marianne Smith, who has lived in the San Francisco Bay Area for over thirty years. She studied literature at Pitzer College in California and in France, and holds an M.A. in Creative Writing from San Francisco State University. She has published fiction and nonfiction prose, edited manuscripts and books, and worked as a communications professional in education and the arts. "Walking Distance" originally appeared in *Subject to Change,* a limited edition anthology by the Oakland Community Memoir Project, funded by Cal Humanities, Director Frances Lefkowitz (Paper in my Shoe Press, 2015).

Benjamin Greenspoon is student at Roosevelt High School in Seattle, WA. He loves playing and watching sports. He continues to volunteer with the Student Conservation Association. He lives with his mom, younger sister, and two pets, a cat and a dog.

Laura Hart is a writer, reader, thinker, and belieber. After moving from her small hometown of Skaneateles, NY, she's now a marketing manager currently trying to hack it in New York City. She's a cat fanatic, an extroverted introvert, and deeply values wearing warm socks. You can find her (and her cat) on most social media outlets as @LauraHart7. Her work has previously appeared in *Lake Region Review* and Shade Mountain Press's *The Female Complaint*.

Donna Hilbert's latest book is *The Congress of Luminous Bodies*, from Aortic Books. *The Green Season* (World Parade Books), a collection of poetry and prose, is available in an expanded second edition. The work about the death of her husband appears in *Transforming Matter* and in *Traveler in Paradise: New and Selected Poems*, from PEARL Editions. Her work is widely anthologized, including in *Boomer Girls, A New Geography of Poets, Solace in So Many Words*, and most recently in *The Widows' Handbook* (Kent State University Press), and *The Doll Collection* (Terrapin Books). She lives in Long Beach, California. More at www.donnahilbert.com.

While Christina (Debbie) Hinman was venturing around the globe, her career in international education took her to live on almost every continent. In Uruguay, she met a courageous and visionary Irish monk who had other plans for his life, which he felt included her. After ten years of living large and loving greatly, Debbie was widowed in Ireland from her beloved Edward in 2002, just after their son's fifth birthday. She and her son, Nicholas, now live in the robust and stunning Pacific Northwest. Her work was published in the poetry book, *Liberty's Vigil: The Occupy Anthology: 99 Poets Among The 99%*.

Azim Khamisa is an inspiration. Hailed by dignitaries such as the Dalai Lama, Former President Bill Clinton, and Al Gore, Azim carries his inspirational message of forgiveness, peace, and hope into a world in desperate need of each. Following the loss of his only son, Tariq, in 1995 to a senseless, gang-related murder, Azim chose the path of forgiveness and compassion rather than revenge and bitterness, and this amazing choice led to the establishment of the Tariq Khamisa Foundation (www.TKF.org) and the subsequent forgiveness movement, which has reached millions.

G. Elizabeth Kretchmer earned her MFA in Fiction from Pacific University. The author of two full-length works—*The Damnable Legacy*, a novel, and *Women on the Brink*, a short story collection—writes about many of the losses and other unwelcome realities women face in today's society. Her short fiction, essays, and creative nonfiction have appeared in the *New York Times* and other publications. Ms. Kretchmer regularly facilitates creative and wellness writing workshops for survivors of cancer, domestic violence, and brain injuries; stressed-out corporate employees; yoga practitioners; and others. For more information, visit her website at www.gekretchmer.com.

Judith Strauss Leader has been creating stories since she learned to talk. Always fascinated by people and the ways they interact (or don't), she has written short stories, live theatrical performances, screenplays, television shows, magazine articles, and children's stories. A happy wife (her supportive husband understands her belief that housework can wait), proud mother, teacher, active member of her synagogue, and community volunteer, a busy Judi cherishes her time with friends, whether playing Mah Jongg, drinking champagne, cooking together, or walking in the woods. Something she does not understand is how our resource-rich world allows people to go hungry.

Corbin Lewars is a developmental editor and writing consultant residing in Seattle, WA. She is the author of PNBA and Washington State book awards nominee *Creating a*

Life: The memoir of a writer and mom in the making (Catalyst Book Press, 2010) and *Divorce as Opportunity* (Booktrope, 2014). She is currently working on *God's Cadillac,* a story of love, friendship, and talking trees. Her personal essays have been featured in over twenty-five publications including *Mothering, Hip Mama,* and the *Seattle PI* as well as in several writing anthologies. She has been teaching writing for over twenty years in a variety of settings including universities, writing conferences, homeless shelters, CEO boardrooms, prisons, Seattle Cancer Institute, and the Richard Hugo House. For more information, visit www.corbinlewars.com.

Jenny Cutler Lopez is a freelance writer based in Northern Virginia. Her nonfiction writing appears in publications such as *East City Art, Hippocampus Magazine, Kurt Vonnegut Memorial Library Journal, Split Lip Magazine,* and *Northern Virginia Magazine.* She won the 2014 Howey Award for Best Nonfiction Book for *Who I Am: American Scar Stories,* which profiled Northern Virginians through the use of short essays and photography. Connect with her at jennycutlerlopez.com and IG @slowmoscorpio.

Ann Mayo resides in Coquitlam, BC, and is a rarity in that she is one of very few area inhabitants who were born and raised in Vancouver. She is very involved with the environmental movement, the Canadian Reiki Association, writing poetry, volunteering, and her garden. Her work background was mainly in counseling but Reiki 'called' to her, and she now runs a mobile Reiki business in Burnaby and Coquitlam. One of her favorite hobbies is spinning dog fur and raw silk into yarn, and she has been known to play the Queen on occasion.

A resident of NY, Stephen Mead is a published artist, writer, and maker of short-collage films and sound-collage downloads. His latest P.O.D. Amazon release is an art-text hybrid, *According to the Order of Nature (We too are Cosmos Made),* a work which takes to task the words which have been used against LGBT folks from time immemorial. In 2014 he began a webpage to gather links of his poetry being published in such zines as *Great Works, Unlikely Stories, Quill & Parchment*, etc., in one place: *Poetry on the Line*.

J. R. Miller was born and raised in the blue-collar suburbs of Detroit. After a career designing and copywriting for a large advertising agency in metro Detroit, he moved to Florida, where he received his MFA in Creative Writing from the University of South Florida. He is the author of *Nobody's Looking* (ELJ Editions 2015). His work also appears in *The Good Men Project, Midwestern Gothic, Palooka, Writers Tribe Review, Portland Review, Prime Number*, and others. You can visit his website at www.miller580. com.

Aubrey Montoya is proof that being a teenage mother does not have to ruin your life, for, in fact, it saved her life. While raising her amazing son X-Zavian, who is now seventeen months old, she was able to continue high school, where she is currently a senior, and now works at Sweeto Burrito. She lives in Utah with her grandparents and ball of joy, X-Zavian. She hopes to continue writing and plans on writing her own book on being a teenage mother.

Florrie Munat has worked as an English teacher, a reference librarian, and a Young Adult book reviewer. Her nonfiction articles and stories for children have been published in magazines such as *Cricket* and *Highlights for Children*, as well as Microsoft's *My Personal Tutor* software. Her memoir, *Be Brave: A Wife's Journey Through Caregiving*, describes her experience of caring for her husband, Chuck, who had Lewy body dementia. Learn more about Florrie and *Be Brave* at www.florriemunat. com.

Jennifer D. Munro's blog, StraightNoChaserMom.com, won First Place in the National Society of Newspaper Columnists contest. She was a Top Ten Finalist in the Erma Bombeck Humor Competition. Her writing has appeared in numerous publications, including *Salon; Full Grown People; Best American Erotica; The Bigger the Better the Tighter the Sweater: 21 Funny Women on Beauty and Body Image; and Tarnished* (Pinchback Press), in which a version of this essay originally appeared. She is a freelance editor living in the Pacific Northwest, where she also teaches at writing conferences and literary centers. Website: www.JenniferDMunro.com.

Patricia A. Nugent's creative nonfiction stories have been published by professional and literary journals and won an award bestowed by Susan Sontag. She authored a collection of vignettes about adult parental loss entitled, *They Live On: Saying Goodbye to Mom and Dad*. Her play, *The Stone that Started the Ripple*, has been performed numerous times to sell-out crowds. Retired from school administration, she has been an adjunct professor, volunteers to teach creative writing to lifelong learners, and periodically blogs for *Ms. Magazine*. However, it is her role as caregiver at the end of her parents' lives of which she is most proud.

Toti O'Brien was born in Rome and lives in Los Angeles. Her work has appeared in *Syntax & Salt, Wilderness House, Litro UK*, and *Entropy*, among other journals and anthologies. Translations of her poems have appeared in Serbian literary journals, and she has contributed to various Italian magazines. More about her can be found at www.totihan.net/writer.

Judith Pacht's *Summer Hunger* (Tebot Bach) won the 2011 PEN Southwest Book Award for Poetry. Her chapbooks, *User's Guide* and *St. Louis Suite* (Finishing Line Press), were published in 2009 and 2010. Her first chapbook and poetry collection, *Falcon*, was published in 2004. A three-time Pushcart nominee, she was first place winner in the Georgia Poetry Society's Edgar Bowers competition. Pacht's work has been published in journals that include *Ploughshares, Runes, Nimrod*, and *Phoebe*, and her poems were translated into Russian, where they appeared in *Foreign Literature* (Moscow, Russia). Pacht taught Political Poetry at Denver's annual LitFest at the Lighthouse.

A rural Wisconsin-grown homesteader and former New Yorker, Leona Palmer received a degree from NYU's Gallatin School in post-colonial women's literature. She cofounded Curves for Change, a nonprofit promoting positive body image for girls and women. Currently she is the content specialist for the Omega Women's Leadership Center at the Omega Institute for Holistic Studies. She is a regularly featured contributor to *RoleReboot.org, The Huffington Post,* and *HandpickedNation.com,* examining media representation, women's health, and sustainable living, and has a food blog with her partner at 20boxes.tumblr.com, featuring Ironwood Farms. She lives in Hudson, NY, and is finishing her first book, a memoir and social critique about death and grieving.

R aj Persaud retired in 2012 from a long and successful information technology career in Canada. In that period, she had written numerous materials on application of technology use in business, but she always wanted to write a book. A lover of both classic and modern literature, Raj wrote her first book in 2014. *Living with Purpose: Pt Sirju's Spirited Journey* details her father's incredible life of service. This *JALMT* essay is her second published work.

D iana Raab, Ph.D. is an award-winning author of eight books and over 600 articles and poems. She's a memoirist, poet, blogger, essayist, and educator. She is an advocate of writing for healing and transformation. She's been writing since the age of ten, when her mother gave her her first journal, to cope with her grandmother's suicide. *Lust* is her most recent poetry collection. Her book, *Writing for Bliss: A Seven Step Plan for Telling Your Story and Transforming Your Life,* is forthcoming in 2017. Raab is a regular blogger for *Psychology Today, The Huffington Post,* and *PsychAlive.* Her website is dianaraab.com.

K ristin Bryant Rajan is a PhD in English, with a focus on Virginia Woolf and an interest in the nature of identity in modernist literature. She currently teaches at a community college in Atlanta, GA, and enjoys writing fiction, poetry, and creative nonfiction. Her writing can be found in: *The Watershed*

Review, The Explicator, and the anthology *Moon Days: Creative Writing about Menstruation,* among others, and she was recently chosen as a 2016 Pushcart nominee. She finds writing to be an extension of her daily meditation practice, opening her awareness to the wonders of each day.

Dave Reeck is a father, tinkerer, family cook, and cyclist. An annual adventurer, he can be occasionally found on top of mountains, bike packing across countries, or walking in the wilderness. He enjoys making great experiences into great stories. He's currently engaged in a multi-year adventure called "raising a family."

Sierra Rigdon is a writer at heart who has been through tremendous ups and downs from a young age. These experiences have led her to write about her life—both to help others who have been in a similar situation and to heal herself. She is currently working on several short stories and hopes to one day publish a novel. She graduated from high school and lives in a drug-free environment. From Sierra: "I truly hope you can't relate to my story, but, if you can, I want you to know that you are not alone and it is not your fault. Speak up and speak out. Get the help you need and heal yourself, because you deserve it."

Sherry Rind is the author of four collections of poetry and editor of two books about Airedale terriers. She has received awards from the National Endowment for the Arts, Anhinga Press, Artist Trust, Seattle Arts Commission, and King County Arts Commission. She teaches at Lake Washington Institute of Technology.

Josh Salmon recently graduated high school and is figuring out what comes next. After writing this, he gave his father another chance and this time wasn't disappointed. His relationship with his dad is developing into something of its own, and he is okay with that. He lives in Utah with his mother and pit bull, Roxi, and spends his free time with his girlfriend or playing video games.

Terry Severhill has appeared in a variety of journals, including: *Damnfino, A Quiet Courage, Soul-Lit,* and others. He is the recipient of the Art Young's Good Morning Memorial Award for Poetry, 2016 (Garbanzo Literary Journal). He has appeared in five anthologies, is scheduled for publication in three more in 2016-17, and has several more poems waiting to appear in various other journals. Born in the north woods of Upper Michigan, he is part Chippewa, part Scot, part Marine, and ALL American. He resides in Vista, San Diego County, CA, where he writes, and he reads at several open mic venues each month. When not writing or loafing or gardening, he volunteers at a homeless/marginalized shelter.

Sally Showalter is an emerging writer and has studied fiction writing at Center for Creative Writing Works in Tucson and The University of Arizona where she received a Certification in Creative Writing. Some of her fiction has appeared in Summer Shorts II, an anthology of short stories and poetry in Festival Writer. She was an active member of a bi-monthly writers' group for fourteen years who are currently working on a book of their collective writings. Showalter continues working and writing with diverse talented writers in various workshop settings in Arizona and other states.

Chaya Silberstein has been published in *The Pen Name* and *The Venice Beachhead.* She writes for *Poetry Salon* and has kept a blog since 2005, www.eatingpoetry.com. Under this umbrella, she "serves" Poetry Cookies at events throughout Los Angles, which have included The Abbot Kinney Festival with Beyond Baroque and the Venice Arts Council. Nicknamed "The Roving Poet" by Art for All People, she has brought poetry to their many events throughout California. She has been part of Public Works Improvisational Theater's "Voice in the Well" Literary Salon since 2013. She is the co-author of *The Echo of Dreams,* a collaboration of poetry and photography. She currently resides in Venice, CA.

Will Silverman began writing poetry at the age of twelve. Despite working a variety of jobs and "career" paths, Will has consistently returned to writing as an outlet for his soul. In poetry, he enjoys the challenge of evoking emotions using strong, descriptive words in an efficient manner. Will spent his early years on the East Coast, but finally found home in Montana. Drawing inspiration from mountains, Will has spent thirty-eight years in Missoula searching for passion in the beauty of his surroundings. He studied writing under Richard Hugo at the University of Montana. Will earned a bachelor's degree in creative writing and also holds a master's degree in public administration. Will derives his greatest inspiration, however, from his children, Malia and Koby. Through them, comes light, love, and tremendous joy.

Meghan Skye lives in Northwest Washington.

Dr. Sharon Stanley has educated professionals internationally in the principles and practices for healing the effects of grief, loss and trauma. Building on her research on empathy, Sharon founded Somatic Transformation, a psychotherapy model and professional curriculum. ST is based on emerging research in developmental neuroscience and offers a phenomenological approach to restoring vitality and meaning following overwhelming experiences. Sharon's book: *Relational and Body-Centered Practices for Healing Trauma: Lifting the Burdens of the Past* was published by Routledge in 2016. Sharon has a clinical practice and small training center on Bainbridge Island, Washington. www.somatic-transformation.org

Bret Stephens, winner of the 2013 Pulitzer Prize for commentary, is the foreign affairs columnist and deputy editorial page editor of *The Wall Street Journal*. He was previously the editor-in-chief of the *Jerusalem Post* and has written for *Foreign Affairs and Commentary*, among other publications. He lives in New York City.

Lee Karen Stow entered journalism in 1989, traveling on assignment to around sixty countries, documenting people and places for national newspapers, magazines, and books, including *The Times of London, The Daily Telegraph, BBC In Pictures, Wanderlust,* and *CNN Traveller.* Since 2007 she has devoted her time and skills to the pursuit of long-term solo projects on contemporary women's issues, including: *42 Women of Sierra Leone* and *Poppies: Women, War, Peace.* In 2012 she was awarded an Honorary Degree (Doctor of Letters) by the University of Hull, UK, for photographic work. She is Honorary Research Fellow at WISE (Wilberforce Institute for the Study of Slavery and Emancipation), University of Hull. www. leekarenstow.com.

Ann Teplick is a Seattle poet, playwright, prose writer, and teaching artist. She writes with youth in hospitals, psychiatric units, juvenile detention, public schools, and arts non-profits. She's received funding from Artist Trust, Seattle Office of Arts and Culture, 4Culture, and The Society of Children's Book Writers and Illustrators. She is currently working on a collection of poems, *Snapped into Fractions,* which reflects her twelve years writing poetry with youth in psychiatric facilities.

Mary Langer Thompson's poems, short stories, and essays appear in various journals and anthologies, most recently Altadena Poetry Review. She is a contributor to two poetry writing texts, *The Working Poet* (Autumn Press, 2009) and *Women and Poetry: Writing, Revising, Publishing and Teaching* (McFarland, 2012). She was the Senior Poet Laureate of California for 2012. A retired public school principal and former secondary English teacher, Langer Thompson received her Ed.D. from the University of California, Los Angeles. She lives in Apple Valley with her husband, Dave.

Emilie Winthrop had a long career as a Parsons-trained Interior designer and closet writer until her husband's death from Alzheimer's and cancer, when she changed careers to become a feature writer and theater critic for San Diego magazines, then executive editor of *SD Decor* and *Style* magazine. Now confined to a wheelchair, she lives with her Tibetan Spaniel in Carlsbad, CA, where she recently finished a memoir cookbook on the glory days of Leadville, Colorado's silver rush, and is currently working on a mystery novel. She firmly believes in counting your blessings, writing every day, and NEVER retiring.

Loraine Wolff was a single mother of two boys for ten years. She worked long retail hours and was in charge of her life. When she met Frank, she had no idea what it felt like to fall so completely for someone. She realized that although she had her cake, he put the frosting on it. Boating, fishing, and being outdoors were her new playground. She says, "He treated me like I walked on water. When he talked about me to others, I was embarrassed. No one could be as awesome or accomplished as he made me sound. I still cannot believe that I was so very much loved by such an amazing person."

Lyndee Yamshon obtained her PhD in creative writing from UIC's Program for Writers in 2015. Publications include *Wreckage of Reason II: Anthology of XXperimental Women Writers, Eckleburg Review, China Grove Literary Journal, Packingtown Review, The Chicago Tribune, Bookslut,* finalist status from Glimmer Train for her short story "Yoga Barbie," and upcoming fiction in FYIPets Journal. In her spare time, she enjoys chasing her cat Shmick and writing music.

CPSIA information can be obtained
at www.ICGtesting.com
Printed in the USA
LVOW12s2308110517
534233LV00001B/19/P